COMMON SENSE GLOBAL INVESTING

Maurice K. Thompson

Dearborn
Financial Publishing, Inc.®

Editorial Director: Cynthia A. Zigmund
Managing Editor: Jack Kiburz
Project Editor: Trey Thoelcke
Interior Design: Lucy Jenkins
Cover Design: S. Laird Jenkins Corporation
Typesetting: Elizabeth Pitts

Library of Congress Cataloging-in-Publication Data

Thompson, Maurice K.
   Commonsense global investing : how to successfully navigate the international marketplace / by Maurice K. Thompson.
     p. cm.
   Includes index.
   ISBN 0-7931-2962-1
   1. Investments, Foreign.   2. Portfolio management.
   3. International finance.   I. Title.
   HG4538.T466   1998
   332.67′3—dc21   98-9937
                                                   CIP

Dedication

This book is dedicated to the memory of Robert E. Spear, whose uncommon common sense, good humor, and understanding heart made him truly at home in the modern world. The spirit of humanity has been greatly diminished by his departure.

◆ CONTENTS ◆

◆ PREFACE ◆

The collapse of Asian financial markets in 1997 painfully demonstrated the interdependence of economies throughout the world. How investors reacted to the calamitous events reflected their various levels of sophistication. Most sold all of their foreign securities. Others acted like Chicken Little and, thinking the sky was falling, sold everything, even the industries basic to their own economy. In the United States, fear that the "Asian flu" would infect America triggered a sharp sell-off, stripping 1,200 points from the Dow Jones Industrials in a few weeks. This fear was not irrational, but the reaction of many investors was extremely irrational.

This book provides a basis for rational behavior. Although the Western stock markets have recovered from the Asian shock and proceeded to set new highs, many investors have begun to wonder how long the good times can last. Bargains have disappeared and it has become increasingly difficult to find good values in the U.S. market. If you are one of those who think the U.S. market is overvalued, now is a good time to consider the values available in other areas of the world. The U.S. economy has enjoyed a decade of sustained growth, but Europe is only now showing signs of a healthy expansion. Asia remains in the throes of recession. Opportunity for gains lies in the neglected markets of the world. Benjamin Graham, the father of fundamental investment analysis, pointed out that the largest gains are not made by the buyers in bull markets; they are made in bear markets, although those investors do not know it until later.

Based on your temperament and desires, the recommendations in this book will point you toward the investment areas most suitable for you. The first two chapters reveal the more important aspects of world economic and political systems. Chapter 3 demonstrates how commonsense economics can help you determine which countries offer the best likelihood for successful investment.

Chapter 4 provides a simple key for determining your tolerance for risk. That self-knowledge should serve to keep you out of positions that lead to sleepless nights, and direct you to investments that can be evaluated without emotional involvement. Scared money makes for poor decisions. Chapters 5 through 8 cover the basics of how you can invest in the global market.

Speculation is always intriguing because of the large profits that may result, but it also carries the attraction of forbidden fruit when the potential for disastrous losses is not considered. Chapter 9 differentiates between speculation and investment. This should help you understand the basics of currency trading explained in Chapters 10 and 11. Even if you never participate in options or futures, knowledge of how such markets work will help you to analyze the flow of capital around the world.

Chapter 12 is a summary of the main points of the book. A glossary defines abstruse terms, and the appendixes provide a ready reference of facts about each area of investment mentioned in the book.

Good luck in becoming a successful international tycoon.

◆ ACKNOWLEDGMENTS ◆

This book consists of the slow accretion of knowledge acquired from thousands of sources throughout my career in the securities business. I wish that it were possible to acknowledge each contribution, but that is impossible. Instead, I pass along the knowledge in the form of this book. I hope that others may be helped as I have been.

I wish to thank all of the people directly responsible for the production of this book, especially the following: Cynthia A. Zigmund, editorial director at Dearborn Financial Publishing, Inc., was an enormous help in the organization of amorphous ideas into comprehensible units. John Kellam, Commodity Futures Specialist with A.G. Edwards, Palo Alto, California, provided up-to-date material on the currency futures markets. Trisha Kramer, BT Alexander Brown, San Francisco, California proved invaluable in checking information from all areas of the investment world. And Frederick J. Yeager, Dean Witter Reynolds, San Mateo, California, provided expertise in the area of investment trusts and closed-end funds.

CHAPTER 1

The World Is Your Oyster

The Trick Is Learning How to Shuck the Thing!

On July 2, 1997, few U.S. investors regarded the collapse of the Thai bhat with much more than bemused interest; one of the Asian tigers, and a minor one at that, had finally caught its tail in a wringer. However, as succeeding waves of currency devaluation swept over adjacent countries, complacency gradually turned to terror. The currency collapse spread like a fever from Thailand to Malasia, Indonesia, and the Philippines. It swept through Singapore and threatened China and even steadfast Hong Kong.

The advantages of investing in foreign markets continued to be touted by an ever-increasing volume of advertising from many sources, as though nothing had happened. Clever TV spots trumpeted the expertise of international fund managers; mailings solicited subscriptions to market letters from unknown gurus promising guidance; and brokers interrupted your dinner, each claiming to have the best international research.

Who can you believe? All of those people were telling you to spread your investments globally, to be an active participant in the world markets. Should you have? Within the next four months, the advertising for mutual funds disappeared and U.S. holders of closed-end trusts and mutual funds that concentrated on the tiger economies of Asia bailed out, losing as much as 50 percent on their investments. Only those who recognized the tell-tale signals from the currency markets were able to preserve their capital before the panic began.

You will find answers to many of your questions about the mechanics of global investing, including the role played by currency markets, in this book. A knowledge of market mechanics, however, will not be enough to ensure success. Investment strategies, tailored to individual needs, must be employed if the rewards from global investing are to be collected and dangers avoided. Unfortunately, no book can provide a magic formula for wealth. Although entry into international markets has become easy, no strategy yet devised can replace your own good judgment.

Thirty-five years of condensed, investment experience has been organized to provide you with the knowledge necessary to profit while others panic. You will also find that several time-honored precepts of investing are questioned. Common sense must outweigh any maxim when it is your money at risk. Each chapter deals with a particular segment of international investing. Consideration is given to the advantages and disadvantages of each area, always with the hope that knowledge of the various investment avenues will lead you to the one that will serve you best.

Diversification Is the Refuge of the Timid

Diversification can reduce investment risk by offering the probability that a bad investment will be compensated for by a good investment. The broader the diversification, the more likely this will be true. Diversification, when properly applied, permits the investor to participate in a variety of profit centers. However, fear of losses has driven many investors to embrace the diversification concept to the exclusion of common sense. Overdiversification ensures the inclusion of poor investments, and can only result in mediocre portfolio performance. Some people have been known to hold a dozen or more mutual funds, even though each mutual fund is comprised of a diversified portfolio. Diversification, for its own sake, should be the least of your reasons for investing in overseas markets!

Opportunity Is Reason Enough

Fifty years ago, stocks traded on U.S. exchanges represented over 75 percent of the world's economy. Today, this figure has been reduced to less than 40 percent. Fifty years ago, an investor could afford to ignore 25 percent of the world's business enterprises and still find excellent opportunities. Now, the investor who refuses to look beyond the United States is ignoring more than 60 percent of the opportunities. Study the world and diversify your opportunities. Emerging markets represent many countries, some that have patterned their securities markets in the manner of Western economies and some that have not. Markets that are open to foreign investors offer liquidity and fair pricing. Markets that limit the access of foreign investors create special problems of liquidity and pricing. Free markets represent an enormous step forward in facilitating the flow of investment capital to areas of opportunity (see Figure 1.1).

The Global Viewpoint

To take advantage of the enormous change from many isolated economic systems to a single global economy, you must adopt a new way of looking at things. You are fortunate to be alive during this time of change—a change more sweeping than was the change from farms to factories. This change offers enormous opportunities for accumulating wealth. Your job may disappear tomorrow, but if you understand how the economics of the world interrelate, your future is secure. Watch for the liberalization of restrictions on foreign

FIGURE 1.1 Emerging Markets, Restrictions on Foreign Investment

Free Market	Some Restriction	Heavy Restrictions
Chile	Argentina	China
Hong Kong	Brazil	India
Mexico	Czech Republic	Peru
Nigeria	Indonesia	Poland
South Africa	Israel	Russia
	Malaysia	Sri Lanka
	Pakistan	South Korea
	Philippines	Taiwan
	Singapore	Uruguay
	Thailand	

investment in the emerging markets. These may offer some of your best opportunities (see Figure 1.2).

Change is always a threat to those enjoying a comfortable status in life. Many see change as a malevolent force conceived by evil men and look for scapegoats instead of opportunity. They see imported goods displacing domestic products, immigrant labor taking the jobs of American workers, or overseas factories paying low wages as a cause for the decline of American heavy industries. Politicians wrap these fears in the flag and call for the United States to withdraw from contact with the outside world. In short they would return to the "good old days" and the isolationism of the 1930s. You must ignore these cries of despair and listen to the sound of money swiftly flying around the world.

As conglomerate nations splinter into a myriad of new nations, the first badge of sovereignty is a new currency. (The list continues to grow. Appendix H provides a list of currencies as of 1997.) Estonia, Latvia, and Lithuania quickly introduced their own currencies when they broke away from the Soviet Union in 1992. Armenia, Georgia, Moldova, Turkmenistan, and the Ukraine quickly followed

**FIGURE 1.2 New Issues from New Markets
(Emerging Market Equity Issues)**

Country	U.S. $ Value (millions)	Country	U.S. $ Value (millions)
Argentina	4,142	Mexico	11,200
Bangladesh	26	Morocco	8
Brazil	1,220	Pakistan	1,188
Chile	1,161	Panama	559
China	5,713	Peru	159
Colombia	305	Philippines	1,886
Czech Republic	42	Poland	15
Estonia	4	Romania	1
Ghana	398	Russia	48
Hong Kong	1,827	Singapore	1,643
Hungary	310	Slovak Republic	113
India	3,833	South Africa	598
Indonesia	2,044	Sri Lanka	33
Israel	1,212	Taiwan	1,058
South Korea	2,266	Thailand	1,712
Liberia	207	Uruguay	23
Malaysia	438	Venezuela	188

Source: IMF Statistical Summary 1996. Data from 1991–1995.

suit. Russia now uses a ruble bearing the imprint of the Bank of Russia rather than the USSR.

Instant worldwide communication has been the prime cause behind the disintegration of multiethnic nations. By linking all of mankind within a single worldwide knowledge network, the individual has been liberated from depending on a national government to supply news and information. Even news and information a national government might seek to suppress is now available to those who really want the truth.

News of the rise of a communist party in Nepal, an earthquake in Chile, or the share price of a Swedish company traded on the Japanese stock market has become a part of everybody's life. How a nation reacts to these changes will determine its destiny and the well-being of its citizens for generations to come. To know how to access and use this information will determine the prosperity of individuals.

Valid Assumptions Require Valid Data

Or, as Mark Twain put it, "It ain't so much the things that people don't know that makes trouble in this world, as it is the things that people know that ain't so."

The millennium is at hand. Fantasies of what the twenty-first century will bring are being replaced with objective projections. Although these projections are based on the realities of today, they all carry the biases of the individual making the predictions. How accurate any projection turns out to be is dependent on the accuracy of the perception with which today's reality is assessed. In a time when information can be instantaneously transmitted to any part of the world, the validity of the information may not be scrutinized as carefully as was done in the past. Economic data obtained from the Internet, where even the most backward countries seem to have Web pages, should be considered suspect. Remember, even reports from sources such as the U.S. government on matters of unemployment, GDP (gross domestic product), corn supply, etc., are usually revised several times before a final figure is agreed on. Forecasts based on data from the initial releases may be quite misleading and costly if used to make business decisions.

Reports from other countries on similar matters often are based on little more than wishful thinking, or, occasionally, outright fraudulent reporting. Some of the more reliable Web site addresses are listed in Chapter 3. To use unsupported data in any investment decision translates in computerspeak to "GIGO," garbage in—garbage out. This potential for error may be of minor importance in everyday life; however, it can be of infinite importance when making an investment decision.

To begin a book with such a caveat may seem strange, but it is done to emphasize the point that in the universe of investment possibilities, there are no constants, only variables. Indeed, even the decision to invest at all represents a variable that can alter the course of a life, or in the aggregate, the fate of a nation. Knowledge is the key to success in the global economy, but if that knowledge consists of invalid data, its use can only lead to disaster.

Using the Currency Key

The relative strength or weakness of a currency reflects the relative strength or weakness of an economy. This provides a useful tool in assessing the validity of other information collected about a foreign economy. However, using the relative strength of a currency as the single key to successful global investment is a trap to be avoided. Intervention in currency markets by a government to support (peg) its currency may result in a false valuation for that currency. Too often we look for simple roads to success in a complex world. Judging the strength of a currency should be only the final step in your assessment of the potential rewards of any foreign investment.

Why Countries Act the Way They Do

Today, nations are, for the most part, the products of past political decisions. Their boundaries were set to achieve political goals rather than to adhere to natural geographic formations or ethnic relationships. Such artificial boundaries can be maintained only through overriding economic benefits to the citizens or through military force.

Changes of either economic or military forces can have a devastating effect on such politically inspired nations. Recently, we have seen the separation of Pakistan from India, the disintegration of the Soviet Union, the destruction of Lebanon, and genocidal warfare in the Balkans. In each of these cases, the desire of the individual citizen to be affiliated through ethnic or religious, rather than economic, ties resulted in the breakup of politically dictated nations.

Present day China represents a case where economic welfare is perceived by the citizens in the provinces to warrant their continued affiliation with the national government and their support of national armed forces capable of maintaining political boundaries and internal security. The economic powerhouse of Hong Kong was placed under the sovereignty of China on July 1, 1997, but was allowed to keep the Hong Kong dollar as its currency. The maintenance of this sound currency should be uppermost in the aims of the Chinese government, but how long the politicians in Beijing will withstand the temptation to raid the Hong Kong treasury remains an open question (see Figure 1.3).

Nations governed by ideology rather than economics are viable only so long as the citizens are adequately fed. Should the economic benefits of maintaining a central government become less obvious to the majority of citizens, that government is likely to be replaced. China could easily follow the course of the Soviet Union into dissolution if its economic plans falter.

A basic pattern has emerged: Nations that for political purposes are a federation of diverse ethnic groups are likely to be divided into those separate ethnic nations. Such realignment of nations is not new, only the speed of such dissolution has changed. The Ottoman Empire once stretched from Vienna to Bombay and took centuries to break up, while the disintegration of the Soviet Union took only a few years; Yugoslavia was dissolved in a matter of days (see Figure 1.4). As W.B. Yeats wrote, "Things fall apart; the center cannot hold; . . . anarchy is loosed on the world."

This basic pattern can be traced through all the seeming chaos: A strengthened allegiance to ethnic groups is replacing nationalism based on political boundaries. Knowledge of this pattern will help reduce political risks when making investment decisions. This explains why Singapore investments are politically safer than those

FIGURE 1.3 China, the Amazing Conglomerate Nation

Province	Area (1,000 sq. km)	Population (est.) (1990 census in 1,000)	Separate Language*
Hebei	202.7	60,280	yes
Shanxi	157.1	28,180	no
Liaoning	151.0	39,980	yes
Jilin	187.0	25,150	yes
Heilongjiang	463.6	34,770	yes
Jiangsu	102.2	68,170	no
Zhejiang	101.8	40,840	yes
Anhui	139.9	52,290	no
Fujian	123.1	30,610	no
Jiangxi	164.8	38,280	no
Shandong	153.3	83,430	no
Henen	167.0	86,140	no
Hubei	187.5	54,700	yes
Hunan	210.5	60,600	yes
Guangdong	197.1	63,210	yes
Hainan	34.3	6,420	yes
Sichuan	569.0	103,370	yes
Guizhou	174.0	32,730	yes
Yunnan	436.2	36,750	yes
Shaanxi	195.8	32,470	no
Gansu	366.5	22,930	yes
Qinghai	721.0	4,430	yes
Autonomous regions			
Inner Mongolia	1,177.5	21,110	no
Guangxi Zhuang	220.4	42,530	no
Tibet	1,221.6	2,220	yes
Ningxia Hui	170.0	4,660	no
Xinjiang Uighur	1,646.8	15,370	no

*The ideographic writing system (revised to contain only 2,000 characters) is in effect throughout China. Because each character represents an idea rather than a sound, printed matter is understood by everyone despite the barrier of differing languages.

in China, and those in Botswana politically safer than those in South Africa. Of course, there is more to successful global investing than judging the political risks involved.

Of the many ways to judge economies of countries, some criteria are obvious: Only a fool would invest in a country torn by civil war. Other criteria may be so obscure that only a diligent search will reveal them. Wishful thinking and intuition are never to be trusted. Remember, an investment in a country facing bankruptcy offers little chance for success.

Commonsense Investing Tips

- Global investments are successful in direct proportion to the knowledge on which they are based.
- No matter how much you learn, you will never know all there is to know about any investment. An investment must be based on foresight, derived from knowledge fitted into a pattern.
- A currency that is "pegged" to the dollar can mask mischief. Watch for changes in foreign reserves whenever a currency is tied to the dollar.

Because every investor differs from every other, two keys are provided in Chapter 4 to aid you in determining your own investor profile. The first key reveals the degree of personal involvement you are willing to bring to the selection of investments. The second key determines your risk tolerance level. Knowing your risk tolerance level is most important if you are to avoid sleepless nights. After all, the purpose of attaining wealth is to give you a carefree life. What is the point if the process produces worry and anxiety?

Just as it was said in ancient times that all roads led to Rome, you will find that all of the methods discussed in the following chapters ultimately lead to the same destination: a safe haven for your savings and a reasonable return on your investments related to the risks you are willing to take.

FIGURE 1.4 New Nations Formed in the Second Half of the 20th Century

New Nation	Old Name/ Colony	New Nation	Old Name/ Colony
Afghanistan	Soviet Union	Mauritania	French Colony
Algeria	French Colony	Mauritius	British Colony
Angola	Portuguese Colony	Mongolia	Soviet Union
Bahrain	British Protectorate	Mozambique	Portuguese Colony
Bangladesh	Britain/India	Nambia	South Africa
Belize	British Colony	Pakistan	British Colony
Belarus	Soviet Union	Papua New	Australian Protect.
Bosnia	Yugoslavia	Guinea	
Botswana	British Protectorate	Poland	Soviet Union
Czech Republic	Czechoslovakia	Russia	Soviet Union
Democratic	Belgian Colony	Rwanda	Belgian Colony
Rep. Congo		Senegal	French Colony
Gabon	French Colony	Seychelles	British Colony
Gambia	British Colony	Sierra Leone	British Colony
Georgia	Soviet Union	Slovakia	Czechoslovakia
Ghana	British Colony	Slovenia	Yugoslavia
Guinea	French Colony	Sri Lanka	British Colony
Guyana	British Colony	Sudan	British/Egyptian
India	British Colony	Suriname	Netherlands Colony
Indonesia	Netherlands Colony	Swaziland	British Protectorate
Israel	British Protectorate	Tanzania	British Colony
Kampuchea	French Colony	Tonga	British Protectorate
(Cambodia)		Turkmenistan	Soviet Union
Kenya	British Colony	Tuvalu	British Protectorate
Laos	French Colony	Uganda	British Colony
Latvia	Soviet Union	Ukraine	Soviet Union
Lesotho	British Colony	Vanuatu	British/French Prot.
Lithuania	Soviet Union	Vietnam	French Colony
Malawi	British Protectorate	Zambia	British Colony
Malaysia	British Colony	Zimbabwe	British Colony
Mali	French Colony		

◆ **FABLE** ◆

The True Facts about the Three Little Pigs

The old sow had grown tired of her rambunctious offspring. She gave each of the three brothers a piece of gold, told them to go and seek their fortunes, then kicked them out of the house. At first, this was upsetting to the three little pigs, but when they reached the village, they were overcome with excitement. They saw turnips by the sack-full, and boxes filled to overflowing with beautiful golden carrots. It was almost more than a hungry pig could stand.

"Let's get a bag of turnips," said the first pig. "They cost only one gold piece."

"I like carrots better," said the second pig. "They cost three gold pieces for a full box, but if we put all of our money together, we could buy them."

"And what would we do after we had eaten them?" asked the third little pig. "We must save our money to use wisely while we seek our fortunes."

Such wisdom was not lost on the first two little pigs. They saw that their brother would be a constant pain in the neck, so when he suggested that they go down the road past the village, they said in unison, "Oh, no. That's too dangerous. We'll seek our fortunes in this village." With that, they turned their backs on their brother, leaving him to wander down the road alone.

With the third little pig gone, the two little pigs set out to explore the village. They stopped in front of a building and read the sign on the door—A. Wolff, Real Estate. "I've heard that fortunes are made in real estate," said the first little pig. "I'm going in to see what it's all about."

Inside, he was greeted by a well dressed fellow with slick black hair and glittering eyes. "You're in luck," the man said. "We have some really fine specials today. How much money do you have?"

"I have a gold piece," said the little pig.

"Oh my, you really are lucky. I have just the thing for you. A lovely plot of land, with plenty of straw for building a house. Once your house is built, you can rent rooms and make a fortune."

"Really?"

"You have my personal guarantee, and its all yours for just one gold piece."

The little pig gave the man his gold piece and scampered out to tell his brother that his fortune was made. "I'm going to see if I can do the same thing," the second little pig said, as he went into the office.

Unfortunately, the land with enough straw to build was all sold, the man explained. However, there was a plot with plenty of sticks, and sticks can make a very fine house. "How much?" the second little pig asked.

"How much do you have?"

The little pig showed his gold piece to the man.

"Oh, you are so lucky," the man said. "It's yours for just one gold piece."

The two little pigs trotted off to build their houses on their land. This is when the trouble started. You see, where people have hands and feet, pigs have only trotters. If you have ever tried to bundle straw together for thatch, using only a trotter, you will understand the problem. And, if you think bundling straw is a problem, try weaving sticks with a trotter! The pigs sat forlornly amidst the sticks and straw, wondering what to do. Then the first little pig remembered. "Mr. A. Wolff gave his personal guarantee. Let's go get our money back."

But, when they returned to the village to get their money, the sign on the door of the real estate office had changed. It now read A. Fox, Real Estate. Inside the office they found a sleek fellow with

red hair and eyes that seemed to glitter like those of A. Wolff. Mr. A. Wolff was gone and Mr. A. Fox had no idea where he could be found. The two little pigs returned to their land to wait for their brother. They huddled on a sorry bed of straw with a meagre fire of sticks to ward off the cold evenings, and with the melancholy thought that one did not have to be a sheep to be fleeced.

Weeks later, the third little pig found them lean and famished. From his knapsack he produced bunches of fresh carrots. While they greedily feasted, he brought forth another surprise, a bag full of gold pieces. "How did you do that?" the two little pigs asked.

"I used my gold piece to buy two bags of turnips in the village. Then I took them to the seaport at the end of the road where the ships come full of carrots from far lands. They can't grow turnips there, although carrots off the ships are cheap. I sold each sack of turnips for a piece of gold, then I bought two boxes of carrots for each gold piece. That gave me four boxes of carrots. These, I carried back to the village, where I sold each for three pieces of gold. If you are willing to join me, we could all make our fortunes in the trades."

So the Pig & Bros. Trading Company was founded, and soon the three little pigs were able to buy the biggest brick house in the country.

Moral: The grass always looks greener on the other side of the fence; and sometimes it is.

World Trade 101—How the World Works

The worldwide economic expansion of the 1990s has not bene-fited all people equally. This fact has been used by the detractors of capitalism to press for more of the same government intervention in the flow of trade that is largely responsible for the disparity in economic growth. A quick study of those countries that have pro-gressed most rapidly produces a list of nations that have elected to support privatization of industry over state control. A list of those countries that have made the least progress in improving the living standards of their citizens reveals the heavy hand of central control over production and trade. Whether the country is organized polit-ically as a democracy or as a totalitarian state seems to have far less impact on the economy than does the level of governmental control over the means of production.

Two examples will serve to illustrate the power of free enter-prise. Fifty years ago, India was freed from colonial status and, fol-lowing the teachings of the London School of Economics, promptly nationalized the country's means of production. At about the same time, China became a totalitarian socialist nation, as prescribed by Karl Marx. Neither made much progress until China moved away from total central control a decade ago and began to permit small

FIGURE 2.1 Emerging Markets, China and India

Growth in Gross Domestic Product 1985–1995 (U.S. $1,000)		
	China	**India**
1985 GDP	896,440	2,622,430
1995 GDP	4,500,580	7,863,550
Per Capita Growth		
1985–1995	5.6%	2.2%

Source: United Nations Statistical Yearbook, 1996

cottage industries to develop free of government intervention. India, however, stayed the socialist course. The results are startling: Totalitarian China now shows a doubling of per capita income for the past 50 years, while democratic India shows an actual decline in per capita income over the same period (see Figure 2.1).

Economists are still divided in their opinions as to the proper balance of state control and free market forces that will produce the most good for the most people. The "American" model depends on economic forces and a flexible labor force to determine the most fruitful employment of capital. Although this system seems to produce an ever-growing economy, it is at the cost of an increasing inequality of living standards between the trained (educated) and untrained (uneducated) workers. In contrast, the "European" model, with its inflexible labor regulations and government support of the unemployed, results in increased unemployment as the price for wage equality between the trained and untrained.

The most successful economies in the future will probably be those that follow the idea of flexible labor but attack the wage differential problem through education of the workforce. A workable system of education is part of the social infrastructure so important to the viability of any economy. The availability of such training to all citizens is one of the most important criteria in determining whether a country warrants investment consideration.

The ability of a government to change its economy is enormous, but its ability to change the economy for the good is usually overestimated. Government actions, however noble in purpose, often have an opposite, unanticipated reaction. Interference in the basic supply/demand equation, whether for labor or goods, is often undertaken by governments to correct perceived faults in the free market system. Monopolies are protected from overseas competition by restrictive tariffs or the setting of quotas. Minimum wages are legislated to improve the conditions of the working poor. Price support for agricultural products is seen as a method of preserving small farms and an idealized way of life. Each of these interventions results in unintended reactions. The protected monopolies produce goods and services at a higher cost to the citizens; minimum wage laws price some untrained workers out of the labor market; and agricultural supports, like monopolies, increase the cost of living for all.

Perhaps the most costly intervention of all is when governments seek to cover their inadequacies by restricting the free flow of capital and trade. Economies of underdeveloped countries are often retarded by an overzealous attempt at industrialization. Steel mills, chemical complexes, cement factories, and even automobile plants are funded without thought as to where markets exist for the goods produced. In trying to force an agrarian economy into the 21st century, politicians often opt for the visible structure rather than concentrating on measures, such as education, that will provide for a gradual increase in the country's quality of life.

Adam Smith (*Wealth of Nations*) introduced the idea of a productive advantage; that is, if one country is very good at making shoes and another is very good at producing wheat, it is to the advantage of each to concentrate on what it does best and trade for what it does poorly. Thus markets for both shoes and wheat are increased, benefiting both economies. This simplistic view is misleading. Leaders of an undeveloped country with an unproductive economy can only despair when all the world seems to do everything better. Trade barriers go up in hopes of protecting the inefficient local producers from the importation of cheaper and often better quality foreign goods. Aid from developed countries is quickly squandered on futile social programs or make-work projects with little hope for any real improvement of the economy. The country stagnates. Politicians must learn that in the long run, no economy is harmed by free trade.

It is difficult to stamp out the idea that an economy may be harmed by free trade. Even in the well-developed United States, debates over ratification of the North American Free Trade Agreement (NAFTA) treaty propelled a little-known financier to high visibility when he contested the benefits of free trade. The heart of the debate was the fear of exporting jobs, rather than goods, and that the standard of living is somehow decreased through the import of lower-cost products.

Environmentalists have joined with the isolationists in opposing free trade. Again it is a lack of understanding that propels their argument. The Sahara Desert is expanding, not through lack of rain, but because its peoples are destroying arable land in an effort to obtain their next meal. Efforts of the World Bank, the Peace Corp, and UNESCO have failed so far to halt this environmental degradation. The rain forests of the world are likewise facing destruction at the hands of subsistence societies just trying to stay alive. The practice of slash-and-burn to obtain fertile land has been around since man first discovered fire, but it can no longer be tolerated. In 1997, the entire Indonesian area was blanketed for weeks by a pall of smoke so dense as to threaten the health of millions of people. Today, the destruction of the environment is largely the result of desperate people who, facing starvation, regard the sacrifice of a few trees as unimportant. Free trade provides that important alternative. Free trade is environmentally neutral and should not be held hostage or used as a lever in the solution of social problems.

Totally ignored in the NAFTA debate was the concept of *comparative advantage.* David Ricardo, a 19th-century economist, first advanced the idea that a country could advance its economy if it concentrated on producing the goods in which it had a comparative advantage. His assumptions were as follows:

1. Even a country that was worse at producing everything than every other country in the world and thus had no absolute advantage over any other country could still benefit from trade.
2. Such a country would still find that it was more efficient in producing some goods than in producing other goods.
3. The goods produced most efficiently had a comparative advantage over those produced inefficiently.
4. Such a country would still prosper by the production and sale of goods in which it had a comparative advantage.

The confusion lies in thinking that a country must have an absolute advantage in producing some good over another country for trade to be beneficial. It is the production of goods that have a comparative advantage over other goods that determines the likelihood of success.

Commonsense Investing Tips

- Invest in countries that are reducing barriers to international trade.
- Invest in countries that are privatizing government businesses.
- Invest in countries that are expanding public education.

◆ **FABLE** ◆

The Way the World Works

The Princess of Drow was in despair over her poor country. The finance minister had done all he could to protect the farmers and cobblers from unfair foreign competition. He had placed a 100 percent tariff on all goods entering or leaving the country, but collected nothing. As no one would pay the tax, the treasury grew as lean as the countryside.

Even the farmers who worked from dawn to dark complained that, although prices for grain had improved, so had prices for everything else. It still took three bushels of grain to buy a pair of shoes. The cobblers complained that, although there was no competition from cheap foreign imports, the price of food had risen so fast that they could sell their shoes for only three bushels of grain.

The princess traveled to the neighboring kingdom of Orcim to seek a remedy for the malaise affecting her country. There she met a handsome prince (but more about that later) and a wise financial minister. She learned that the farmers of Orcim were happy that prices for grain were so high that a pair of shoes could be purchased for a single bushel of grain. The cobblers, of course, had to work from dawn to dark just to put bread on the table. The wise finance minister said that he could not make everyone happy, but if the two countries would open their borders to free trade, everyone would be better off.

This sounded like nonsense to the princess. How could trade change the lot of anyone, let alone improve the lot of everyone? She looked at the handsome prince for answers, but he only winked and tapped his head with his forefinger. He too thought the minister was talking nonsense.

"Let me explain," the minister said.

"If you can," the handsome prince muttered.

"Please do," requested the princess, who was much too polite to be rude.

"Let us assume," the minister began, after the manner of economists, "that Orcim currently produces seventy bushels of grain for every thirty pairs of shoes. If we turned the cobblers into farmers and stopped making shoes, we would produce one hundred bushels of grain. Of course, we could not eat that much. On the other hand, if we stopped farming and made everyone a cobbler, we could produce one hundred pairs of shoes. Of course, we would never wear that many."

Orcim was indeed a rich country the princess thought, as she compared the minister's statistics to those of her country. In Drow, the farmers produced barely two bushels of grain for every three pairs of shoes the cobblers turned out. Her people were always a little hungry, but at least everyone had shoes. She knew that even if she turned every cobbler into a farmer, they would gain only one additional bushel of grain, and everyone would be barefoot. On the other hand, if she turned every farmer into a cobbler, they could produce three times as many shoes. Her head began to swim. "Could you explain how this concerns Drow?" she asked.

"Perhaps a small chart would help," the minister said as he laid a sheet of paper on the table and began to write. "This is where the two countries are now."

	Grain Production (bushels)	Shoe Production (pairs)
Orcim	70	30
Drow	20	30
Combined Totals	90	60

"We're such a poor country," the princess sighed.

"And this is how it would look if each country produced only what it did best." The minister drew another chart.

	Grain Production (bushels)	Shoe Production (pairs)
Orcim	100	0
Drow	0	90
Combined Totals	100	90

"But my people would starve," the princess cried.

"Let's go back to the first chart," the minister said. "See, in Orcim they have a choice of producing either 100 bushels of grain or 100 pairs of shoes, so we can say that one bushel of grain equals one pair of shoes."

The handsome prince was looking bored.

"In Drow, where they can choose to produce either 25 bushels of grain or 90 pairs of shoes, we can say that one bushel of grain equals about three and one-half pair of shoes."

The princess smiled for the first time in days. "I see," she said. If everyone made shoes, we could trade each pair for a bushel of grain from Orcim and still have plenty left for ourselves."

The minister had one more chart to make. "This is how the two countries would prosper if each shifted to the product in which it has the comparative advantage."

	Grain (bushels)			Shoes (pairs)		
	Produced	Consumed	Excess	Produced	Consumed	Excess
Orcim	100	70	30	0	30	0
Drow	0	20	0	90	30	60
Totals	100	90	10	90	60	30

The princess was ecstatic. "Everyone would be better off. We could eat more, wear more shoes, or sell the excesses to some other country."

The handsome prince was dazzled by the radiant princess. "Will you marry me, so that we can live happily ever after?"

The princess, of course said no. She went back to school to take her doctorate in the source of her new-found love—economics.

Moral: To prosper, a country should concentrate on what it does best, and trade for that which it does less well.

◆ CHAPTER 3 ◆

Factors in Choosing the Best
Countries for Investment

Trying to Find the Safest Country for an Investment May Seem Like Trying to Find the Leader of a School of Sardines

There are certain basic legal concepts for a governmental structure under which investment can flourish. These factors are often overlooked or taken for granted by citizens of the Western democracies. The first of these is the right to own property. Without the right to accumulate, develop, and transfer property, an individual has no incentive for investment. Ideally, the legal system of a country should guarantee all aspects of this right, not only to its own citizens but to foreigners as well. Investors rushing to partake in the vast new markets of China and Russia are relying entirely on the promises of reform by governments to ensure property rights. Unfortunately, these are governments that are capable of reneging on those promises at any time. Investment in any country that does not respect the property rights of individuals must be considered to be gambling. Remember, the sin for which Cuba is still being punished by the United States was not Cuba's embrace of communism but the confiscation of U.S. citizens' private property by the Cuban government.

A second basic requirement before investment in a country's industry becomes attractive is the right of the investor to withdraw profits at any time. To Americans, 1,000 Bangladesh Taka that cannot be converted to dollars are of little use unless they plan to vacation or reside in that country. A freely convertible currency is one of the prime criteria of an overseas investment. Many governments seek to maintain the stability of their currencies by restricting the outflow of capital. History reveals that in the past, even the mighty United States has resorted to limiting the number of dollars its citizens could take abroad. This power of governments is one of the most restrictive factors in the flow of development capital to Third World countries; for as Mark Twain said, "I'm less interested in the return *on* my capital as I am in the return *of* my capital."

Another important consideration is an impartial court system wherein foreigners are accorded a fair hearing, whether the dispute is with citizens or even the government itself. A court system that cannot find its government to be in error will have equal difficulty in ruling against its citizens in favor of some foreigner, despite the merits of the case. You must invest with extreme caution in newly liberated or developing nations, because they have no history of a strong court system that is independent of the government.

The ability of a country's banking system to operate free of political control is taken for granted by citizens in most western nations, but it is still a novel idea to people in many other parts of the world. Thailand, Malaysia, and Indonesia provided a practical lesson in the need for banking systems free of political control. In each of these countries, the banks were required to make loans to friends and relatives of the controlling politicians with little consideration for creditworthiness. The resultant expansion of their economies was dubbed a "miracle," and other emerging nations were urged to follow their lead. Ultimately, economies built on expanding credit issued without sound collateral, are doomed to collapse and the Tigers of southeast Asia proved to be no exceptions. (This is a lesson that should be learned by political forces in the United States who would interfere with the independence of the Federal Reserve System.) Whether the strong arms of the International Monetary Fund and World Bank will bring about recovery through the establishment of independent banking systems in Southeast Asia is still in question.

Commonsense Investing Tips

- Invest in countries with legal systems that guarantee property rights of foreigners equal to those of citizens.
- Invest in countries where the banking system is independent of the government.
- Invest in countries with the least restrictive policies for withdrawal of funds.

Both China and Russia have elected to move toward the privatization of industries, but in different ways. Russia moved in one bold step to distribute ownership in its factories to its citizens. Everyone of voting age received scrip that was convertible into shares of ownership. With only the oldest citizens (born before 1920) able to remember how private enterprise was supposed to work and with no legal or financial infrastructure in place, it is no surprise that over 90 percent of the ownership shares ended up in the hands of former *nomenklatura* or Politburo members.

China has taken a much slower route. The state still owns all of the major factories, and has set no timetable for distributing ownership to the people. Instead, the central government has moved toward legal and financial structures that encourage the formation of privately held industries. This process will undoubtedly be accelerated under the influence of Hong Kong.

Other desirable conditions are a stable government, a growing economy, and a strong currency. No currency is completely immune to the inflationary pressures of the world economy. Even the Swiss, those paragons of fiscal rectitude, have seen the value of the Swiss franc reduced by half in terms of the goods it will buy over the past 50 years. The flow of dollars into Europe following the inception of the Marshall Plan inevitably inflated the Swiss currency despite the severe controls imposed on the Swiss banks. When holders of dollars sought the safety of the Swiss banks, they increased the reserves of those banks. The conversion of U.S. dollars to Swiss francs required the issuance of additional Swiss francs, increasing the money supply with no increase in the productive capacity of the country. An increase in money without a concomitant increase in production produces inflation. Thus, the United States actually exported its inflation to the Swiss.

Today, the electronic transfer of funds can reduce a country's reserves, or increase them faster than a central bank can take action to stabilize its currency. There is no safe haven from inflation. The best we can do is to identify those economies that are becoming stronger and to avoid those thats are growing weaker. The trick is to liquidate investments in a weakening economy before the weak become truly sick.

A Weak Currency Does Not Guarantee a Weak Securities Market

Often a weak currency will attract investments of strong currencies because real estate or security prices may seem to be bargains when translated into the stronger currency. This phenomenon was quite apparent during the 1980s, when the relative strength of the Japanese yen fostered major purchases of U.S. real estate and the stocks of U.S. corporations by the Japanese. This bolstered the U.S. markets despite a weakening dollar.

There Is No Correlation between Short-Term Security Prices and Currency Direction

Although a weak currency does not always produce a weak securities market, does a strong currency always guarantee a strong securities market? No study to date has revealed any correlation, either positive or negative, between stock market performance and currency valuation. Another look at the yen/dollar relationship of the early 1990s demonstrates this point. The dollar weakened while the stock market showed strength. When the dollar strengthened in 1996, the stock market soared to new highs. Why, then, even bother with currency valuation when making an international investment?

When a Currency Is Strong, Inflation Pressures May Seem to Be Controlled

One of the chief benefits to a national economy of a strengthening currency is the masking of inflationary pressures. A strong currency means cheap imports. True, it also means a lowering of export sales and an increase in the trade deficit, but to the general population, the cheap imports provide a lowered cost of living. You have only to look at the U.S. economy during 1996–97 to see an example of this mechanism at work. The dollar was strong, trade deficits widened, inflation seemed to be in check, the economy was buoyant with the stock market making new historic highs. The citizens of the country thought they had found a new economic paradigm of perpetual prosperity.

It Is Often Better to Make a Mediocre Investment under the Umbrella of a Strong Currency Than It Is to Make a Good Investment, Only to See the Gains Buried under a Collapsing Currency

Denominating your investments in terms of an appreciating currency will not remove market risk from the investment, but it may alleviate the pain from a poor investment when the returns are translated back into dollars.

Confusion is the normal state in the spot currency markets, where news events from every country are immediately known to traders throughout the world. No item, however insignificant, seems to be overlooked by the international information system called the Internet. A trader must respond instantaneously to everything, from a report of a political coup in Ghana to a rumor of an oil strike in Tasmania, if he hopes to scalp a few one-thousandths of a penny profit. Billions of dollars will change hands with the stroke of a computer key in response to such news. Hot money flows like quicksilver, always seeking the highest rate of return with the lowest risk. The savvy investor must learn to ignore the noise from such transactions. These minute-to-minute trades are best left to arbitrageurs, and it is only their cumulative effect over a period of time that has meaning for the investor.

The value of any currency depends entirely on the faith of its holder in the credit worthiness of the issuer, and the participant in foreign markets must be alert for any news that might impact that faith. Sensational events such as earthquakes and political assassinations will make feature stories on the evening TV news, but an increase in the GDP (gross domestic product) of Belgium will not be mentioned. Even news from such major economic powers as Japan and Germany is glossed over lightly when a direct impact on U.S. citizens is not readily apparent. Thus events like the collapse of the Mexican peso in early 1995 come as a surprise to the average person, and explanations of the likely impact on the United States are usually as simplistic as they are wrong.

The mismanagement of an economy cannot be long hidden, but it is often ignored by the popular media. One must learn to sift the news for information of other economies. Often it will be obscured in a comparison with some statistic about the U.S. economy. For example, a report on the U.S. current account trade balance might also reveal the figures for Japan. Don't be too harsh on the popular media for not providing such information in a readily assimilated format; therein lies your opportunity for profit.

Economic Blocks

The economic world seems destined to polarize into three trading blocks, each block dominated by the currency of its strongest country. Countries of Western Europe, including Russia, are well on the way toward unification of a defined trading area, as are the countries of North and South America. The third trading area is less well defined, but will probably evolve in such a way as to encompass all of the Asian countries and India. The interbanking ties within this block were demonstrated too well by the quick spread of economic crisis from Thailand to Korea in late 1997.

Australia, New Zealand, and the South African nations are too far apart geographically to form a fourth trading block, and so each nation will find it necessary to become an ancillary member of one of the major trading blocks. The Arab states seem to be locked in a bitter cultural clash, with no resolution in sight. Until such time as their people recognize the benefits to be derived from peaceful interaction with others, these countries, along with those of central Africa, will continue to occupy peripheral positions.

Which Comes First? The Euro or the Deutsche Mark?

In 1999 Western Europe is scheduled to adopt a single currency, the euro. Before such a currency can be adopted, each member nation must put its financial house in order. Stringent requirements limit the amount of national debt that can be carried as a percentage of a nation's gross domestic product. In efforts to meet this requirement, many European nations have been selling assets such as gold reserves and government owned businesses, using the proceeds to reduce the national debt. Others are relying on creative accounting. All of this bolsters the suspicion that adoption of the euro may be postponed. Until such a currency becomes a reality, the euro serves more as an accounting standard than a currency. Europe will continue to use the German mark as its reserve monetary base. Even after adoption, despite French dreams to the contrary, the Bundesbank (central bank of Germany) will continue to dominate the euro's valuation relative to the rest of the world.

The Dollar's Domain

The second area, encompassing North and South America, will remain dependent on the U.S. dollar for the immediate future. However, in the decades ahead, it is entirely possible that Brazil, Chile, or Argentina may supplant the United States in the Latin American countries, leaving only the North American continent within the U.S. sphere of influence.

The Tigers

The third block is presently in a state of transformation as it becomes liberated from the other blocks. The Japanese yen would seem to be the logical currency to serve as the trading unit, but Japan has carefully managed its monetary supply in such a way as to limit the quantity of yen to an amount just sufficient for internal use. Collectively, the eastern republics of the former Soviet Union have the potential to become dominant powers, as does China if it learns from Hong Kong. But these countries are under considerable stress as they adjust from socialist into capitalist states. None of the other nations comprising the eastern block seem to have the resources to become dominant in the area; so the U.S. dollar will probably continue as the reserve currency for at least the next decade.

The Proximity Factor

Within the trading blocks, political and economic influences radiate from the country that produces the reserve currency for the block. This influence can be plotted on a scale that shows diminishing strength as distance increases from the center. Thus, we see Austria and Switzerland, which are adjacent to Germany, strongly influenced by their powerful neighbor, while France is less inclined to follow the German lead. Sometimes a disciple is more fanatical about following the precepts of the master than is the master. This is sometimes true of countries as well, so it is no surprise that the Swiss and Austrians are more adamant about fighting inflation than are the notoriously conservative Germans. Often an investment in a satellite country will prove more productive than placing the same funds in the economy of the dominant power. However, before investing in an area or country, you should examine the forces at work on the reserve currency of the block.

If the reserve currency appears to be weakening, in all likelihood the currencies of other countries in the block will also weaken. This simplifies our task by limiting the number of currencies we must analyze before making a decision to invest. An evaluation of the strength of the U.S. dollar in relation to the German mark, the British pound, and the Japanese yen will tell you the relative strength of those currencies, which employ one of the basic three as reserves. To the investor, it is important to recognize which major currency is most closely tied to the country in question if a reasoned judgment is to be made. A strong deutsche mark will lend strength to the French franc and, to a lesser degree, even to the Italian lira. Therefore, if you were contemplating an investment in any western European country, the final outcome is more likely to be successful when the deutsche mark is strengthening.

So, how do you know which part of the world offers the most potential for success when you contemplate investing some portion of your funds? Many indicators have been developed to enable the economist to chart the health of an economy. Let us look at four of the most often-reported measures used by economists to determine a country's prospects: gross domestic product, balance of trade, purchasing power parity, and infrastructure.

Gross Domestic Product

One of the most widely used, the gross domestic product (GDP), purports to measure the collective business activity within a nation by totaling all exchanges of money for goods over a set time. These measures are usually released quarterly, but are stated as an annualized figure. By comparing the sizes of GDP of various countries, one is able to judge the relative size of each country's economy. However, in judging the health of economies, the important figures to compare are the changes of GDP from previous measures. Thus, if the GDP in the United States shows an annual increase of 3.3 percent and the GDP of Germany shows a gain of 1.5 percent, it may be assumed that the United States economy is the stronger.

GDP figures are basic in setting economic policies for all governments, and projections of future GDP become crucial to establishing governmental budgets. Several important measures of economic activity lie within the broad GDP figures. Components available to the forecaster include: industrial production, retail sales, unemployment rate, wholesale prices, consumer prices, interest rates, and wages/earnings. Like the GDP, *it is the magnitude and direction* of the number changes from previous reports that is more important than the numbers themselves.

The Balance of Trade Is Seldom in Balance

Although mercantilism died a natural death when the costs of colonialism exceeded the benefits to the colonial power, some remnants of the theory still cloud economic thought today. The fallacy of a "favorable balance of trade" implies that it is possible to export more than is imported, with the difference accruing as a higher standard of living for the exporting country. If this were so, countries like Japan and Switzerland that must import most of their food, raw materials, and energy would be among the most impoverished nations in the world. Nature always seeks equilibrium, as much in the constant flux of international trade as in the cycling of water from ocean to cloud to snow to rivers and back to the oceans.

To understand the dynamics of international trade, the balance of trade is broken down into two interrelated segments: *current account* (the net difference between exports and imports of goods, expressed in the local currency) and *capital flow* (the amount of local currency derived from foreign sources). Over any extended period, the sum of the current account and capital flow must approach zero or be corrected by a decrease in the standard of living. When the sum is a negative number, the local currency loses value against the currencies of other countries exporting to it. This brings about higher prices for imported goods and a decrease in the demand for the more expensive imports. A government may interfere by supporting the value of its currency, but such support can be temporary at best. If overdone, the ultimate result of unrealistically supporting a currency results in the devaluation of that currency.

Purchasing Power Parity

You will often hear some economic pundit on the evening news claim that the U.S. dollar is either undervalued or overvalued in relation to some other currency. The curious idea that, in a free market, one currency may be "overvalued" stems from the theory of purchasing power parity. To understand the concept, you must assume that a basket of goods consisting of identical items should have equal value in any country. To simplify, let us use the single item—rice. If a pound of rice sells for one dollar in the United States and 130 yen in Japan, then it could be claimed that any deviation of the 1/130 dollar/yen ratio would result in one of the currencies being "overvalued." This sounds logical, but in order for the theory to be of any practical use, the demand for the items in the basket must be consistently equal in both countries. No one has yet come up with such a basket because every society has its own preferences. For example, people in the United States will switch to pasta or potatoes if there is a shortage of rice, while the people in Japan will pay the higher price for their rice rather than accept substitutes. Does 160-yen rice really mean that the U.S. dollar is undervalued? Determining the relative value of a currency through application of the purchasing power parity theory is probably the most unreliable method for determining the probable course of that currency.

Interest Rate Differential

Money seeks the highest interest return as naturally as water seeks the lowest level. If all currencies were exchangeable at a fixed rate, then the country in need of foreign exchange would only have to increase its interest rates to attract funds from all over the world. Often markets will act as though this is the case—but for only a short time. High rates are a self-defeating measure because they can be sustained only as long as the inflow of capital can be put to productive use. Capital inflows in excess of that which can be productively employed become a drain on an economy, costing more in interest than they earn.

When an increase in interest rates is announced, care must be taken to determine the cause before making any investment decision. Rates may be raised to curb speculative excesses in an overheating economy, which would be good for the long-term investor. Rates may be raised to attract capital for improvements to the infrastructure, which is good, or raised to stem the outflow of capital that was being used to support inefficient, nationalized industries, such as Mexico in 1990–95.

Currency Reserves

Currency reserves (hard currency deposits in the central bank) will often provide a measure of economic strength, particularly for second-tier nations. These reserves provide a safety net for a country in times of economic setback. A steadily growing reserve account indicates an expanding economy, while a steadily decreasing reserve indicates an economy that is declining. A good example of this is Thailand. After a decade of growth at 8–10 percent, the government was not prepared for any slowdown. When the economy slowed to a moderate 5 percent growth rate in 1997, the government was determined to defend the stability of the baht at the cost of a steadily declining reserve account. The futility of supporting the currency at artificially high levels became apparent in July of 1997 after a 20 percent decline in the reserve account, and the baht was allowed to float. It quickly sank 25 percent within a few days, before beginning a relentless decline that erased an additional 35 percent of its value before any stability was established.

National Debt

A national debt is not a bad thing. In fact, in the modern world it has become a necessity. The ability of a nation to borrow is the key to the operation of a central banking system—the means by which money supply is regulated and provides the life blood of an expanding economy. No economy can expand with a decreasing monetary base.

Interest must be paid on the national debt, and these payments are a drain on the economy. How much of a drain can be measured by the size of the debt in relation to the GDP of a country. The Maastricht plan for a unified European currency calls for member nations to have a national debt of no more than 60 percent of GDP. Possibly more restrictive, the plan also calls for budget deficits of under 3 percent of GDP. Whether or not the plan will work, it does provide the investor with some guidelines for interpreting national debt figures.

Rates of Employment/Unemployment

Of all statistics released by governments, employment rates are the most suspect when one country is compared with another. Sampling methods vary, and even the definition of employment may be quite different. A 6 percent rate may represent full employment in the United States, but would be an intolerable rate for Japan. Again, the best course for interpreting these statistics is from an internal comparison of one quarter with another, one year to the next, rather than with some other country. As with the GDP figures, it is the direction and magnitude of change from previous figures that give you a key to the economy's strength.

Infrastructure

Even the finest, most efficient factory in the world would be worthless if it lacked power for its operation, or roadways and rails to supply it with raw materials and transport the finished goods to markets. Power and transportation form the physical skeleton on which a modern manufacturing economy depends. Without these two basics, a country must develop special intellectual skills or be relegated to that unhappy designation of impoverished nation. If the capital flow from foreign sources to an impoverished nation is diverted from improving the infrastructure, that is, building monuments and palaces rather than roads, the country can offer little incentive for the investor.

Developed countries are likely to ignore the importance of infrastructure to their own economies. Upgrading the infrastructure is easily postponed under the political pressure for social programs. For example, in the United States since 1950, social programs have increased 300 times as a percentage of GDP, while percentage of GDP spending on roads and bridges has actually declined. After all, roads and bridges cannot vote. If this trend continues, the decline in the quality of the physical infrastructure can result only in a decline in the economy. Where will the money to fund the social programs come from then?

Important as it is, a fine physical infrastructure only supports the social infrastructure. Without a good social infrastructure to run the factories, an economy cannot survive in the modern world. The social infrastructure is a difficult concept to define. It consists of a people's history and cohesiveness, work ethic, educational level, and interest in improving conditions for posterity. The success of the Japanese and German economies following the devastation of World War II was largely the result of their social infrastructures. Both had a well educated, cohesive society that was future oriented. Aid from outside sources was not squandered on improving the immediate state of citizens but was invested wisely in the physical infrastructure.

India, in contrast, did not have a cohesive society after colonial rule was terminated. Resources were spent on a war with Pakistan and on building steel mills without economic transportation to deliver raw materials or finished products. Health care services were overwhelmed by uncounted numbers of people living in squalid conditions, and only the wealthy could afford adequate attention. Education of the masses was ignored, and even the elite had to travel abroad to obtain advanced training from foreign universities. Although this is slowly changing, particularly in the areas of training for communications and electronic specialties, one of India's largest exports remains the export of talented people.

Contrast India with Japan, where all schools are identically equipped down to the last book or paper clip even in the poorest districts. Every student learns that the highest duty to himself, his family, and the nation is to become educated to the best of his abilities. Rather than maintaining a military machine, Japan provides universal health coverage for its citizens. Even if you know nothing else about the two countries, it would be easy to guess which one is most likely to prosper.

The Work Ethic

Much has been made about the concept of "work ethic." To many, this implies the willingness to work to the best of one's ability and the exclusion of all thoughts of personal comfort or desires that might interfere. To others, the meaning may be restricted to "a good day's work for a good day's pay." Wherever job security is guaranteed by either governments or strong unions, the "good day's pay" remains, but the "good day's work" comes to mean only time spent at the workplace. England under the Labor Government of the 1950s demonstrated to the world the sad results whenever government largesse replaces a people's pride in work. The work ethic of a people is an intangible that must be considered, even though it cannot be measured, whenever investments are made.

More Commonsense Investing Tips

- Diversify your foreign holdings in terms of Economic Blocks. A portfolio with holdings in Japan, Korea, and Hong Kong is not well diversified; one made up of holdings in Germany, Chile, and Singapore is better.
- Currency devaluation represents the greatest risk to a foreign investor. Be particularly attentive to changes in foreign reserves when a currency is pegged. If the foreign reserves become exhausted, the peg will come loose, and the currency will suffer devaluation.

Using the Currency Key

"There's small choice in rotten apples," wrote William Shakespeare. History demonstrates that it is the destiny of all currencies to be debased. This has been true from the time golden moons were clipped from the edges of a circular coin to create an octagonal one. Today, central banks can perform the same operation on paper money by substituting a printing press for shears. Inflation is another name for currency debasement and even the most circumspect of governments will find that an occasional dose of inflation is politically necessary.

The price of a currency, like any other commodity, is responsive to the two basic precepts of economics: supply and demand. Supply is provided by a country's central bank in response to the particular politics of the issuing country. Demand is not so easily controlled by an issuing country, because it is a function of perceived relative quality whenever a choice of currencies is permitted. Gresham's law, which states that bad money drives out good, would seem to imply that a currency of a lessor perceived quality would be more in demand than that of a higher perceived quality. Such is not the case. The use of the lower quality currency increases because no one is willing to save a depreciating asset. The money is exchanged for goods as quickly as possible. Conversely, a currency that is perceived to be appreciating in value is likely to be held as a reserve (savings). What Gresham's law really means is that good money is withdrawn from circulation through hoarding, whereas bad money is quickly exchanged for goods and services. Inflation results as prices in terms of the bad money are rapidly increased to compensate for the decrease in the value of the money.

Often, currency markets are surprisingly slow to recognize basic changes in a nation's economy. While they may immediately respond to elections or disasters (sometimes the same thing) with sudden wide swings, long-term trends are not easily changed. To use currencies as a key to investment decisions, it is best to smooth the daily fluctuations by charting weekly figures. The simplest chart that is effective in visually displaying trends consists of plotting a single weekly price on graph paper. On the left side, mark off the dollar cost of a single unit of the foreign currency and date the lines across the bottom. If you are using prices from the newspaper, you will find this price listed as "U.S. $ equivalent." If the quotation is given only in terms of "currency per United States $," it can be easily converted by dividing one dollar by the quantity of the currency per dollar. For example, if the German mark is quoted at 1.7925, the price of one mark is $1 ÷ 1.7925 = 55.79 cents. Pick a day (usually Friday is best because it is given in Sunday papers) and mark your graph each week. After a few months, a discernible trend will appear. Use this trend to confirm the information you have gleaned from other sources.

Useful Periodicals for International News

Daily Publications

Financial Times (London): provides international news, world stock market indexes, and pricing for stocks traded on foreign exchanges. Invaluable for the serious, global investor! (And who can be other than serious when money is at stake?)

The Wall Street Journal (New York): provides coverage of major international news.

Weekly Publications

Barron's (New York): section devoted to overseas markets includes commentary and some pricing of major corporations.

The Economist (London): probably the best single source for insight into economic developments throughout the world.

Useful Web Site Addresses

General Business News

Bloomberg Business News: http://www.nando.net/newsroom/nt/stocks.html

Financial Times (London): http://www.ft.com

Organization for Economic Cooperation and Development (OECD): http://www.oecdwash.org

World Bank Socioeconomic Data: http://library.usask.ca/hytelnet_html/ful030.html

Global Investors Guide: http://www.gigweb.com

Pacific Region Forum on Business and Management Communications: gopher://hoshi.cic.sfu.ca/11/dlam/business/forum

Russia and East European Studies Business and Economic Resources: http://www.pitt.edu/~cjp/rsecon.html

Business Home Pages for Countries

Australia: http://www.csu.edu.au/education/australia.html

Brazil: http://darkwing.uoregon.edu/~sergiok/brazil.html

Canada: http:/www.visions.com/netpages/

China: http://www.ihep.ac.cn/china.html

Germany: http://www.chemie.fu-berlin.de/adressen/brd.html

Hong Kong: http://www.hongkong.org/

India: http://sunsite.sut.ac.jp/asia/india/

Israel: http://www.israel.org/

Japan: http://www.glocom.ac.jp/inforum/ifrm.hp.itg.html

United Kingdom: http://www.britnet.co.uk/

◆ CHAPTER 4 ◆

Measuring Your Investment
Risk Tolerance

How to Use the Keys

A key consists of a series of opposing statements. After reading each pair of these statements, choose the answer that most nearly matches your feelings. There are no "correct" answers. Your choice from each set of questions will direct you to the next set, and ultimately you should arrive at the investments most suitable to your needs and your suitability profile.

Measuring Investment Risk Tolerance

Each of the possible investments or speculations discussed in this book bears a Risk Tolerance (RT) rating. This rating is on a scale of I to V, with I having the lowest volatility and V the highest volatility and therefore the highest risk (see Figure 4.1). The RT ratings have no relationship to the probabilities for either gain or loss from an investment. They are intended only as a guide in determining the probability of your sleeping soundly after making the investment.

FIGURE 4.1 Your RT Rating

Assuming that you are equally qualified for all positions, which job would you prefer?

I. A job that offered a secure future with a good pension and health plan.

II. A job with a small start-up company that offered no pension but had a stock option plan.

If you answered with choice I, continue with the next set of questions in Section I. If you answered with choice II, go to the set of questions in Section II.

Section I: A Secure Job

A. Would you prefer a job with the government (federal or state) where promotions are slow but certain and based on good performance and seniority? If you answered yes, your Risk Tolerance is I. Stop.

B. Would you prefer a job with a large corporation where promotions may depend not only on your performance but also on the performance of your division as well? If you answered yes, your Risk Tolerance is II. Stop.

Section: II: Start-Up Company

A. Would you be content to stay with the company as long as promotions and salary increases are regular, even though the company seems to be stagnating? If you answered yes, your Risk Tolerance is III. Stop.

B. Would you like to form your own company?

1. Only if the financial condition was secure and immediate profits were foreseeable. If you answered yes, your Risk Tolerance is IV. Stop.

2. If the idea seemed sound, you would be willing to sell your house, cash in your life insurance, and use all of your savings, even though the first years would probably mean operating at a loss. If you answered yes, your Risk Tolerance is V.

Now that you have determined your Risk Tolerance, it is a relatively simple matter to determine the investment area that is most suitable for you. The questions in Figure 4.2 will direct you to those areas of international investment that most nearly match your profile of interest. When used in conjunction with your RT rating, the Key to Investment Choices will direct you to the investments most likely to match your needs as well as your preferences (see Figure 4.3).

Commonsense Investing Tips

- Exceeding your ability to handle stress will lead to poor investment decisions. No amount of potential gain is worth a tortured life.
- You should not restrict your investments to only those suitable for your highest Risk Tolerance level. Those rated at lower levels are also suitable.
- Your Risk Tolerance level is not chiseled in stone. It will change as you gain experience and confidence in new markets.

FIGURE 4.2 Your Key to Investment Choices

Section I: Dollar or Nondollar

A. Do you think it prudent to invest some of your assets in non-dollar denominated areas? If you agree, go to the next set of questions in Section II.

B. Would you like some participation in world markets but prefer to keep all of your assets in dollar denominated areas? If your RT is I, go to Chapters 5 and 7. If your RT is II, go to Chapter 6.

Section II: Global Investing

A. Do you like to make all of your own investment decisions? If you agree, go to the next set of questions in Section III.

B. Would you prefer to use professional help with your investments? If you agree, go to Chapter 5.

Section III: Making Your Own Decisions

A. Would you prefer to be directly exposed to currency changes? If you agree, go to the next set of questions in Section IV.

B. Would you prefer to use the foreign equity and bond markets as a proxy for currency changes? If you agree, go to Chapter 8.

Section IV: Exposure to Currency Changes

A. Are you comfortable using leverage, and do you understand that this compounds risk? If you agree, go to the next set of questions in Section V.

B. Would you prefer not to employ leverage? If you agree, go to Chapter 7.

Section V: Leveraged Investments

A. Are you interested in exchanging U.S. dollars for foreign currencies, but lack the time to follow the markets closely? If you agree, go to Chapter 10.

B. Are you able to closely follow the foreign currency markets and willing to close out losing positions, even if the loss on a position may be substantial? If you agree, go to Chapter 11.

FIGURE 4.3 Sample Global Investment Plans (Allocations are based on percentages of total investment funds.)

RT I

All investments in U.S. dollar denominated vehicles

- 40 percent U.S. treasuries, U.S. bank CDs, U.S. government mutual funds
- 40 percent international bond mutual funds
- 20 percent international equity mutual funds

Some investments in nondollar denominated vehicles

- 40 percent U.S. treasuries, U.S. bank CDs, U.S. government mutual funds
- 20 percent international bond mutual funds
- 20 percent selected foreign currency denominated CDs with U.S. bank
- 20 percent international equity mutual funds

RT II

All investments in U.S. dollar denominated vehicles

- 20 percent U.S. treasuries, U.S. bank CDs, U.S. government mutual funds
- 20 percent international bond mutual funds
- 20 percent international equity mutual funds
- 40 percent selected U.S. multinational stocks

Some investments in nondollar denominated vehicles

- 20 percent U.S. treasuries, U.S. bank CDs, U.S. government mutual funds
- 20 percent selected nondollar denominated CDs with U.S. bank
- 20 percent international equity mutual funds
- 40 percent selected U.S. multinational stocks

FIGURE 4.3 Sample Global Investment Plans (Allocations are based on percentages of total investment funds.) (Continued)

RT III

All investments in U.S. dollar denominated vehicles

- 20 percent U.S. treasuries, U.S. bank CDs, U.S. government mutual funds
- 20 percent international equity mutual funds
- 60 percent selected U.S. multinational stocks

Some investments in nondollar denominated vehicles

- 20 percent U.S. treasuries, U.S. bank CDs, U.S. government mutual funds
- 20 percent selected non–U.S. dollar denominated CDs with U.S. bank
- 10 percent international equity mutual funds
- 30 percent selected U.S. multinational corporation stock
- 20 percent selected ADRs

RT IV

Using professional help in selecting foreign investments

- 20 percent U.S. treasuries, U.S. bank CDs, U.S. government mutual funds
- 10 percent international bond mutual funds
- 30 percent international equity mutual funds
- 20 percent regional closed-end trusts
- 20 percent selected country closed-end trusts, or WEBS

Making your own investment decisions

- 20 percent U.S. treasuries, U.S. bank CDs
- 20 percent selected nondollar denominated CDs through overseas bank
- 30 percent U.S. multinational corporation stock
- 30 percent selected ADRs

FIGURE 4.3 Sample Global Investment Plans (Allocations are based on percentages of total investment funds.) (Continued)

RT V

Nonleveraged account

- 40 percent U.S. treasuries
- 25 percent U.S. multinational corporation stock
- 20 percent selected ADRs
- 10 percent forward currency markets
- 5 percent currency options

Leveraged account

- 50 percent U.S. treasuries (may be used as margin for futures)
- 20 percent U.S. multinational corporation stock
- 20 percent selected ADRs and WEBS
- 10 percent currency futures and options

◆ CHAPTER 5 ◆

Help from Professionals— Investment Trusts, Closed-End Funds, and Mutual Funds

Moving out of the U.S. dollar without opening a foreign bank account can be as easy as calling your stock broker. For those with $1 million or more, individual accounts under overseas management may be recommended. For those less fortunate, an investment trust might be the answer. Funds placed in an investment trust are considered by the IRS to be invested in a U.S. corporation. Although the trust itself is committed to invest in securities of another country or area beyond the United States, all gains, losses, and dividends are translated into dollar returns that are reflected in the share or unit price. The U.S. investor buys for dollars and sells for dollars, all through a U.S. corporation. Thus there is no foreign investment to report.

Investment Trusts

Investment trusts are not new. Since humans first emerged from the shrouded mists of prehistory, they have left evidence of cooperative behavior. Indeed, one of the things that sets people apart from other animals is the ability to combine individual assets for the advancement of all. Stone tools were the capital of early man. A stone ax or flint-tipped spear provided the means of reaching a higher level of culture than was possible for those without such tools. No single man could have killed a woolly mammoth. The mammoth was slain by cooperating with others in the clan so that all were able to eat, with time left over to paint on cave walls. The Chinese, to this day, continue to pool assets of related family members into *huais* to facilitate the operation of businesses and the purchase of property beyond the capabilities of an individual. Western civilization produced the formation of guilds in medieval times, again to provide the economics of scale through the union of skills and capital for the benefit of guild members.

Today investment trusts are established to pool the money of individual investors who have a common goal. By joining such a trust, investors obtain the diversification and professional management that otherwise would not be available to them. Initially, each investor contributes the amount of money desired, within the minimum and maximum restrictions set forth when the fund is organized. The prospectus informs the investor of the aims of the fund along with the methods that will be employed by the fund manager in attempting to achieve those goals. This is a very important document, and it should be read carefully before the investment is made.

The pooling of funds by many small investors provides an economy of scale that significantly reduces the costs per dollar of investment. All other things being equal, the larger the fund, the lower the costs. An arbitrary price per share is set by the underwriters during the initial offering, usually $10 per share. (An investor with $1,000 would receive 100 shares.) Following the initial offering, the value of shares will vary from day to day. The net asset values quoted in the newspapers are derived by computing the total value of the trust's assets (market value of all securities plus any cash) and dividing that figure by the number of shares outstanding. This gives the amount each share would have been worth had the fund been liquidated on the valuation date. Do not expect to receive this price when you buy or liquidate. All orders are priced at the net asset value at the close of the day *following* receipt of the order.

Unit Trusts

The *unit trust* (Risk Tolerance I) is usually self-liquidating over a predictable time span. These are usually sold in $1,000 units rather than in shares (hence the name). The funds may be invested in real estate, where an orderly liquidation after the projected time frame may not be possible. The investor is not faced with this problem if the trust investments are made in debt instruments; for example, mortgages. Other unit trusts invest in bonds with a fixed maturity date. These trusts have very low management fees because there are few investment decisions to be made after the initial portfolio has been purchased. Bond investment trusts are particularly attractive to the investor who seeks regular income without the bother of "clipping coupons." Once such a trust is established, no new units are issued, nor are any outstanding units redeemed. Often, the sponsoring broker will try to match requests to sell with offers to buy, but generally such an after-market is very thin. A periodic income check is usually mailed to the investor, and a final check representing net asset value will be mailed on liquidation of the trust. An investor should plan to hold the units until the underlying portfolio matures and the trust is liquidated.

As of this date, few unit trusts based on investments in the foreign bond markets are available to U.S. citizens. 1993 saw the first offering of a global fund based on the equities of telecommunications industries, called the EIF Concept Series Tele-Global Trust. Merrill Lynch, Smith Barney, Prudential Securities, Dean Witter, and PaineWebber have been in the forefront underwriting more of these ventures, so you now have many from which to choose. Watch for more single country trusts to be offered besides those currently in existence. Should you decide to buy into one of the existing trusts, place your order with one of the above underwriters. You will have to wait until some current holder wishes to sell, or a new trust is created. When buying into an existing trust, place your bid somewhat above the most recent net asset value (reported in *Barron's*) and be patient. The liquidity is considerably better for the more recent equity-based offerings, because most have one-year durations; however, the maximum sales charge of 2.75 percent may odd-ffset this advantage, because it is applied each time the investment is rolled over.

Some confusion may result from differences in nomenclature between the United States and Great Britain. In Great Britain, the term *unit trust* is synonymous with the U.S. term *mutual fund*.

The following list is a sampling of the wide variety of unit trusts currently available.

Global Unit Investment Trusts (Risk Tolerance III)

DAF Premier World Portfolio (Equity)

DAF Select 10 Hong Kong Portfolio (Equity)

DAF Tele-Global Trust (Equity)

DAF Select 10 United Kingdom Portfolio (Equity)

DAF Select 10 Japan Portfolio (Equity)

DAF Year Ahead International Portfolio (Equity)

DWR Select 30 Global (Equity)

Closed-End Funds

Like the unit trusts, closed-end funds offer shares to the public on a once only basis. The initial price of the shares is determined by the underwriter. For example, if the fund manager decides that $500 million is the optimum amount required for the enterprise, the underwriter might offer 50 million shares at a $10 price, or 33.33 million shares at $15. After initial costs of the offering are deducted, the remaining pool of money is available to the manager for investment. Because the investment pool has been reduced by the offering costs, the initial asset value of a share will be less than the initial offering price. Usually, it is to your advantage to wait until after the offering has been completed and to buy on the after-market. Shares may sell at a premium over net asset value. More often, they sell at a discount sometime after the initial offering. It is important to read the prospectus and determine the rules under which the manager may invest. Some funds are restricted to single countries, while others may invest in well defined regions comprised of several countries. Still others may invest worldwide at the discretion of the manager.

During the past 15 years, many new closed-end trusts have been formed to provide a simple way for U.S. investors to participate in overseas markets. Because the securities held by the trust are priced in terms of a foreign currency, the U.S. investor has in effect exchanged dollars for a foreign currency. An important factor to consider is whether the manager is allowed to hedge against currency fluctuations. There are times when an overseas market may sell off sharply, yet the fund may show gains due to the strength of the foreign currency. If you are counting on some of your gains to come from the appreciation of a foreign currency vis-à-vis the dollar, the last thing you want the manager to do is to hedge against such movement.

Premiums and Discounts

Another important consideration is the pricing of closed-end trusts: After the initial offering has been completed, no new shares will be sold by the fund, nor will the fund repurchase shares at the net asset value. Shares are bought and sold on the open market, often through a New York Stock Exchange listing. The price of these shares is determined by the amount someone is willing to sell them for and what someone is willing to pay for them. Often the shares sell at a price above the net asset value (premium) or at a price below net asset value (discount). Public enthusiasm for stocks in an otherwise unavailable market (such as Korea) may drive prices to unreasonable premiums. Chasing such issues is a sure way to lose money. Buy only when the premium is less than 5 percent, or preferably at a discount from net asset value. Net asset value is reported weekly by most financial publications (*The Wall Street Journal, Investor's Business Daily, Barron's Weekly,* etc.). Finding the right fund for you is like finding the right marriage partner—so many choices available, so many chances to go wrong. As in marriage, a wrong choice can be very expensive to rectify. Simple answers to complex questions are often wrong: Do not assume that a strong currency automatically translates into a strong stock market. In 1994, the Japanese yen gained nearly 20 percent against the U.S. dollar, yet the Nikkei Index lost over 30 percent of its value in the same period. A strong currency promises only that you will receive a favorable exchange rate for your foreign currency when you exchange it for dollars.

Closed-End Global Funds (Risk Tolerance II)

In general, global funds are nonspecific as to where investments are made. Global funds are able to invest in any country, including the United States, so you may never be certain that your aim of diversifying beyond the American economy will be accomplished. The fund managers may decide that the U.S. economy offers the best potential and therefore liquidate most of the fund's overseas holdings. To guard against this happening, check the quarterly or semiannual reports issued by the fund. The following listing of closed-end trusts is not complete, nor should the mention of any fund be taken as an endorsement of its investment value.

Closed-End Regional Bond Funds (Risk Tolerance II)

Area funds are more restrictive on the managers, generally requiring that a large percentage of the portfolio be invested within a specific region. When considering an investment in an area fund, remember that the area often mirrors the economic progress of the country that controls the currency used for settling trades.

Closed-End Single Country Bond Funds (Risk Tolerance III)

Only the largest of the world's economies are able to produce a debt structure of sufficient size to provide enough bonds to allow the formation of single country funds. Thus, you will find such funds restricted to Great Britain, Germany, and Japan. Faced with such a limited choice, the investor may be better served through an area bond fund.

Closed-End Single Country Equity Funds (Risk Tolerance III)

These funds are required by their charters to invest primarily in the securities of the named country. Generally, less than 10 percent may be held in cash-equivalent U.S. securities to facilitate operation of the fund. The portfolio generally contains shares of the largest and better known companies operating in the specified country. The fund's performance will reflect not only the prosperity of the country, but also the judgment of the fund's management as well. In general, hedging is not used to protect against currency risks.

World Equity Benchmark Shares (WEBS) (RT IV) represent the newest mutation of closed-end trusts. Each of the series is listed on the American Stock Exchange and is structured to represent the equity markets of specific countries. These equity markets are measured by the Morgan Stanley Capital Index specific to each country. Each of the series buys equities in the exact proportion to their weighting within the specific index. The aim is to track the price and yield performance of that index. Several countries restrict foreign ownership of their domestic companies to a limited percentage. Once this percentage of foreign ownership has been reached, foreigners are blocked from further purchases on the domestic exchange. This results in a two-tier market. Foreigners can buy only from other foreigners at prices that are often quite different from those quoted on the local exchange. Where these two-tier markets have occurred, the Benchmark MSCI Indices will employ the foreign market pricing in their calculations to best reflect investment conditions for international investors. Such indices are designated *Free* following the country's name.

These funds do not hedge against currency risks, nor do they use derivatives. However, because they do provide for redemption of aggregations of specified quantities of WEBS by Broker/Dealers, they should track the underlying index fairly closely. Although WEBS have been in existence for only a short time, end of day trading indicates that the variation between closing price and net asset value has averaged less than .5 percent. The greatest variation was in the thinly traded Malaysia WEBS where it was only 1.11 percent. Large premiums or discounts from net asset value seem to be quickly eliminated by arbitrageurs. Thus we have a security that reflects its underlying net asset value like a mutual fund. Unlike a mutual fund that is priced after the close each day, WEBS trades are posted throughout the trading day like other closed-end investment trusts.

Dividends and net capital gains are distributed to the holders of WEBS at least once a year, as required by the rules governing mutual funds. These would closely approximate the yield expected from holding the component stocks if it were not for foreign taxes withheld at the source. All accounting is adjusted from the local currency into U.S. dollars. A weak U.S. dollar increases the yield, and a strong U.S. dollar decreases the yield.

The WEBS listed in Figure 5.1 are actively traded on the American Stock Exchange. Additional WEBS are scheduled for 1998. Up-to-date information about World Equity Benchmark Shares can be found on the Web at http://websontheweb.com/enhanced or by phone at 800-810-9327.

Open-End (Mutual) Funds

The *open-end fund,* more often called a *mutual fund,* offers shares to the public on a continuing basis. The share price is determined by the net asset value to which a transaction fee may be added. A no-load fund will be offered at the net asset value alone, with the transaction fees absorbed by a charge to the fund's operating expenses. The redemption of shares from the public is made by the fund, usually without a transaction fee, at the net asset value. If sales and redemptions are excessive, costs to the fund may be a signifi-

FIGURE 5.1 WEBS Traded on the American Stock Exchange

Country	Ticker Symbol	Country	Ticker Symbol
Australia	EWA	Malaysia (Free)	EWM
Austria	EWO	Mexico (Free)	EWW
Belgium	EWK	Netherlands	EWN
Canada	EWC	Singapore (Free)	EWS
France	EWQ	Spain	EWP
Germany	EWG	Sweden	EWD
Hong Kong	EWH	Switzerland	EWL
Japan	EWJ	United Kingdom	EWU

See Appendix E for examples of Global/International, Regional, or Single Country closed-end funds.

cant expense, reducing the value of the investment to its shareholders. These funds are far more likely to require the manager to hedge against currency fluctuations because all redemptions are made in terms of the U.S. dollar. Few single country funds are currently available to U.S. investors. The flood of redemptions that follow a financial crisis in a single market, as occurred in the Mexican market in early 1995, can restrict the liquidity of the fund. At such times, the fund may temporarily suspend redemptions. If you wish to hedge the dollar against a specific currency through buying a mutual fund, it is best to choose the area fund that encompasses that foreign currency.

It bears repeating that a strong currency does not translate into a strong stock market. Often the opposite case is true, such as in the spring of 1995 when the U.S. market appreciated by more than 12 percent (Dow Jones Industrial Average) while the U.S. dollar depreciated by 15 percent against the Japanese and German currencies. This is a strong argument for the use of professional management.

Appendixes A through D list open-end investment trusts (mutual funds) by type.

◆ FABLE ◆

Everyone knows that you should read the prospectus carefully before you invest in a fund. I paid a price to learn this lesson. In October of 1989, I thought that the dollar was about to decline against the major European currencies. I placed $10,000 in a European Bond fund. The dollar plunged during the following months. By the end of 1990, the Swiss franc had appreciated by 33 percent; the German mark by 26 percent; and even the laggard British pound had gained 21 percent. I was elated for having read the markets so well, but then I checked the price at which I could redeem my fund shares. I was dismayed to find that the net asset value had increased by a mere 3 percent. The fund, as explained in the prospectus, had hedged against a change in the relative value of the dollar. It had effectively "protected" me out of at least a 20 percent profit, but I could blame only myself. The fund had done exactly what the prospectus said it would do.

◆ CHAPTER 6 ◆

Investing in U.S. Multinational Companies

The easiest way to diversify your portfolio with overseas investments is to buy shares of U.S. companies with multinational operations (RT II). Companies such as Dow Chemical, Exxon, and Hewlett Packard derive more than 50 percent of their sales revenues from overseas. If you carefully select 10–15 such companies, your portfolio should be well diversified as to industry and somewhat as to geography. What will be missing is any significant investment in emerging economies.

Diversification Reduces Portfolio Volatility

It is axiomatic that investing in companies serving diversified markets tends to reduce the volatility of earnings and market swings (lower earnings from a weak market may be balanced by higher earnings from a strong market). However, you should not expect the price action of your stocks to be different from the major trend of U.S. stock markets. If U.S. markets decline significantly, your stocks may decline to a lesser degree, but you should expect to lose some valuation.

Nor does investing in a multinational company offer protection against currency swings. In times of a weakening dollar, U.S.-based international corporations tend to show strong earnings, but in times when the dollar is strengthening, earnings may be severely penalized when foreign sales are brought home. At first glance, it would seem that a strong dollar should benefit a company based in the United States, but a moment of analysis will reveal why the reverse is true. When a product made in the United States is sold in Japan, the proceeds from the sale are in Japanese yen. If the dollar is strong against the yen, then fewer dollars are received when those yen are exchanged for dollars. Because the company's accounting is in United States dollars, the sale is recorded in a lower dollar amount, reducing profits. When the dollar is weak, the process of translating foreign sales into United States earnings is reversed.

Hedging May Stabilize Earnings

To offset the effects of currency swings, most multinational companies employ various hedging programs. The success or failure of these ventures is revealed in the annual reports of the companies, usually in the notes under "currency adjustments." To the extent that they are successful, the adjustments will approach neutral. In theory, gains or losses from a weak or strong dollar are offset by losses or gains in the hedging accounts.

Market Risks Remain

If the currency variable is removed or significantly reduced, the earnings of the company will then be a factor only of gross sales and profit margins. The investor's major risk remains how the market will value reported earnings, rather than how well the overseas economies perform. Stock markets tend to fluctuate, sometimes valuing a dollar of annual earnings at $10, and at other times at $20. Some companies that produce undesirable products, such as tobacco processors, always receive a lower market valuation despite large earnings increases from overseas. On the other hand, a soft drink company with expanding overseas markets may find its stock price soaring with a smaller earnings increase. Defense and banking industries may be subjected to the same sort of social judgment evaluation, particularly if their increased earnings are from areas considered hostile to western ethical thought.

Social Factors and Emerging Markets

Social factors must be considered whenever a company makes a new commitment to expand its overseas business. This is particularly important when the expansion is in emerging markets where wage rates are viewed as substandard by United States investors. Well-known brand names such as Nike and Kathy Lee Gifford have demonstrated how quickly a company's sales and reputation can be ruined if the press labels the company an exploiter of sweatshop labor.

Appendix F provides a list of many well-known U.S. multinational companies. Many more could be added each year, but this list should provide a starting place for your investigations. That a company derives over 50 percent of its revenues from overseas operations does not make it either a good or a bad investment. You must first determine whether the overseas operations are in countries with which you are comfortable. Investors in Union Carbide discovered too late that the Indian courts were anything but hospitable to a foreign company when sabotage destroyed the chemical plant at Bophal with horrendous loss of life.

Information Sources

Yearly, detailed reports of operations (K-10s) filed with the Securities and Exchange Commission, as well as annual reports to shareholders, will provide the information you need about foreign operations of a company. Your research will reveal that the majority of international companies derive most of their overseas revenues from only a few countries, primarily those of Western Europe, South America, and the developed nations of Asia. A few others restrict their foreign operations to neighboring Canada and Mexico. Investments in underdeveloped nations are tentative and can take years to become profitable to any significant degree. Even then, the repatriation of profits may be difficult or forbidden. Except for oil, gas, and mineral exploration companies, where the profits may be retrieved through the export of raw materials, there is little corporate investment in developing countries. Therefore, a portfolio comprised of only major international corporations will provide little representation in the potential markets of the under-developed countries, where two-thirds of the world's population lives.

For an easy entry into emerging markets, while keeping all of your funds invested in U.S. corporations, you might consider adding a small percentage of your total investment to a closed-end fund, one that specializes in developing economies. Several of these funds are listed in Appendix E.

◆ FABLE ◆

The Portfolio

Mrs. Senatus arrived for the appointment ten minutes late and took the chair opposite the broker without a sign of apology. She seemed the type of woman a waiter would automatically address as "madam." She sat with both hands clutching the handbag on her lap as she listed her requirements.

"My good friend E. Winthrop Jones highly recommended your services, so I'm sure that you can help me. I have a CD coming due at the end of the month and I'd like to put the money in something more adventurous." She leaned forward as though about to reveal some dark longing. "I want something exotic, perhaps overseas?" Having delivered the message, she pulled back in her chair to observe his reaction.

"How much money are we talking about?"

"Fifty-thousand dollars."

"And what percentage of your total funds would that represent?"

"I see no reason for you to know that." Her tone indicated that his question had bordered on impropriety. "Just say that it's a very small percent. Even so, I don't want anything risky. I don't invest money to lose it."

"Of course not," the broker reassured her. "Have you considered a mutual fund? There are several that specialize in overseas markets."

"They cost too much."

"But, there are no-load funds without a commission."

"I've looked into all that. Their management fees are too high. That's why I asked dear Winthrop to recommend a broker. I want you to work out a portfolio of overseas investments that I don't have to worry about and that I don't have to pay fees on year after year."

The broker was becoming uneasy. What had seemed to be a slam-dunk, when "Win" Jones had made the referral, was taking on the aspects of work. Not just work, but work with little reward in store as far as he could see.

But "Win" was one of his best clients, so he really had little choice. The main thing was to avoid mistakes. A big mistake would lose Mrs. Senatus as a client and, more important, damage his reputation with "Win." Cautiously, he advanced a new idea. "Putting your money in foreign stocks, even ADRs, would cost you a lot in fees, not to mention taxes due foreign governments."

She reacted as though a swarm of flies had landed on her nose. "Taxes to foreign governments? No, I don't want to do that!"

"I could work up a portfolio of American corporations that do a lot of business overseas. It wouldn't be direct exposure to foreign markets, but it sure would simplify things for you."

That seemed more to her liking. "Do that," she said. "I'll pick it up this afternoon."

"I'm afraid it'll take more time than that. I want to be sure that it's well diversified as to industries, as well as being of top quality." She was nodding in agreement, so he continued. "Why don't we get the account open while you're here? Then I can just mail the portfolio to you. After you've looked it over, we'll be all set to go ahead."

Too fast.

"Here's my card," she said. "It has my address and telephone number. You can mail the account papers along with your investment suggestions when they're finally ready." She rose from the chair, extended the card casually between two fingers. As she left the office, she turned her head and said, "Thank you for your time. I'll be sure to tell dear Winthrop how kind you've been."

"Dear Winthrop, indeed," the broker mused as she departed. $50,000 to fit into a safe, diversified portfolio of American companies earning most of their money from overseas. A one shot deal that might bring in two or three hundred in commissions, with his

FIGURE 6.1 The Broker's Dream Table

Company Name	S&P Rating	% Sales Foreign	Industry	Price per share as of 8/30/92	Number Shares	Total Cost
AFLAC Inc.	A+	80%	Insurance	32	150	$4,800
Boeing Co.	A+	50	Aircraft	38	150	5,700
CPC Int'l.	A	60	Foods	24	200	4,800
Coca-Cola	A+	65	Soft Drinks	43	100	4,300
Exxon	A–	63	Petroleum	65	75	4,875
Gillette	A	65	Razors	56	100	5,600
Hewlett Packard	A	52	Electronics	58	80	4,640
IBM	A–	55	Computers	87	50	4,300
Millipore	A	60	Filters	28	150	4,200
Warner Lambert	A–	52	Pharmaceutic	65	100	6,500

take only thirty percent of that. Hours of work ahead, his reputation on the line . . . all for maybe a hundred bucks. Thanks a lot, Win.

Once he started to work on the portfolio, his mood swung back to optimism. This was the part of the business he loved, and he was good at it.

Maybe, when Mrs. Senatus saw how good it was, she would increase her investment. Maybe tell her friends. Anything was possible in the new global economy. Hours later, he put the finishing touches on the portfolio and set it beside his bed, just in case he came up with any changes while he slept. He dreamed of the table shown in Figure 6.1.

He waited a week after mailing the suggested portfolio and account papers before calling Mrs. Senatus. "Do you have any questions? Was there something I left out?" he asked.

"No," she answered, "it was just what I wanted. In fact, I called Winthrop and told him what a fine job you'd done."

"Thank you," he said. "I was wondering . . . I haven't received your account papers yet."

"That won't be necessary now. I followed your recommendations, but I used a discount broker. Much cheaper, you know."

"Yes, I know," he sighed as he lowered the phone onto its cradle.

Except for the nagging little stab of pain that flashed across the back of his neck whenever the words "discount broker" were heard, during the following months, he had managed to shut out the memory of Mrs. Senatus. That is until she unexpectedly called.

"Your IBM, its down to 71. I've lost nearly $800, thanks to your recommendation. What am I to do about it?"

The broker pondered.

"Well?" Her voice lashed his ear like the snarl of a rudely awakened dog.

"I suggest," he said slowly, savoring each word, "that you call your broker." He hung up the phone before concluding, "And 'Dear Winthrop' be damned."

◆

◆ CHAPTER 7 ◆

Investing in Foreign Currency Certificates of Deposit

Bank certificates of deposit (CDs) (RT I) have long been a haven for widows, orphans, and the timid in general. Available in small denominations, they pay slightly higher rates than U.S. government obligations of equal maturity. They are guaranteed to return the full face value, although not the accrued interest, should the bank fail. The Federal Deposit Insurance Corporation (FDIC) covers each account for up to $100,000. For example, were you to place $100,000 in an insured bank CD at 6 percent with a one year maturity, and the bank fails eleven months later, you would receive your $100,000 back, but the $5,500 accrued interest would be lost. You are charged nothing for this insurance. In this example, for simplicity's sake, the interest figure was based on a simple interest for one year. Actually, your bank would more likely have compounded the interest on a monthly or quarterly basis, giving you an actual return of about 6.25 percent. Obviously, you earn more if your bank compounds interest on a monthly rather than a quarterly basis. This should be checked before you invest.

There are other caveats besides the potential for loss of interest. Most banks have a policy for rolling over maturing CDs along with interest. This is a convenient way to compound your funds and, for small accounts, may present no problem other than a change in the interest rate. However, in the case of a $100,000, one-year 6 percent CD, the principal amount to be reinvested will have become $106,000. This is $6,000 over the insurance limit and leaves that amount unprotected. Also, some banks reserve the right to roll over matured CDs into other forms of investment, such as regular passbook savings accounts that pay a much lower rate of interest. It has been reported that one Savings and Loan Bank even moved money from insured CDs into uninsured commercial paper. It pays to read the small print on the papers confirming your purchase of a CD, and to respond promptly with your instructions to the bank at maturity.

It may come as a surprise to learn that many U.S. banks offer Foreign Currency Denominated Certificates of Deposit (RT II). These CDs are purchased with U.S. dollars and the bank will convert the face amount into the foreign currency that you select. Thus, a $100,000 CD may become a 165,000 D-mark CD (more or less, depending on the going exchange rate) if you wish to be in the German currency. Your money is not directly exchanged for deutsche marks, but becomes a bookkeeping entry on the bank's accounts the day of the purchase. The actual purchase by the bank will depend on whether the bank's foreign exchange department is running a surplus or deficit in deutsche marks. In any event, the purchase to cover the bank's liability for your account will represent only a tiny fraction of that day's currency transactions. Buying CDs denominated in a foreign currency is the easiest method available to U.S. citizens to diversify their dollar assets, and like other CDs, foreign currency denominated CDs are insured by the FDIC for up to $100,000 principal amount should the bank fail. The FDIC does not insure against a loss of capital should the U.S. dollar gain against the currency you selected.

For example, suppose that you bought a $100,000, one-year, 6 percent CD denominated in deutsche marks. On the day of purchase, the deutsche mark is priced at 1.6500 per dollar. Thus your CD is booked by the bank as a 165,000 DM credit to your account.

A year later, you would be credited with an additional 9,900 deutsche marks of interest bringing your total account to 174,900 DM. Should you choose to cash out the account and not to roll over, the amount you would receive depends on the going ratio between the dollar and deutsche mark on that particular day. If the rate had remained at 1.6500, your account would equal $106,000. However, had the rate changed in favor of the dollar to 1.7500 per dollar, your 174,900 deutsche marks would be worth only $99,942.86. (A 6 percent depreciation of the deutsche mark in terms of the dollar has absorbed more than the 6 percent interest that you received in deutsche marks.) However, had the deutsche mark appreciated by 6 percent to an exchange rate of 1.5510 over the same period, your 174,900 DM would give you $112,765.96.

From the foregoing, you can see that each percentage change in the rate of exchange versus the dollar results in adding to or subtracting from your capital. Your band of protection is represented by the interest earned on the CD. Unfortunately, the IRS doesn't see this as an interest adjustment. In their eyes, you have been paid 6 percent in interest, which is fully taxable at ordinary income rates. Any plus or minus resulting from currency changes is considered to be a capital gain or loss, and must be calculated separately. The bank will supply you with a breakdown, so don't let the book work stand in your way.

CDs denominated in foreign currencies may be purchased from most large banks, although some are more eager than others for this business. Each bank has its own restrictions and rules applying to the opening of these accounts, so it is best to check thoroughly before you invest. The following list of banks with departments offering foreign currency denominated CDs is not complete, nor is it to be taken as a recommendation, but is merely representative of what is available to the investor.

U.S. Banks Offering CDs Designated in Foreign Currencies

- **Chase Manhattan Bank**
  Chase Manhattan Plaza
  Wilmington, DE 19801
  Telephone 800-242-7365
- **First Union National Bank**
  301 South College
  Charlotte, NC 28288
  Telephone 800-736-5636
- **Mark Twain Bank**
  1630 South Lindbergh Blvd.
  St. Louis, MO 63131
  Telephone 800-926-4922

Brokered CDs

Recently, several brokers have begun offering foreign currency CDs to U.S. citizens. For a small fee, these brokers will arrange a CD with a bank located in the country of your choice. As with the U.S. banks noted above, your funds will be traded for foreign currency and your interest will accrue in that currency. You will be certain of where your account stands only when the CD matures and the funds are exchanged for U.S. dollars. Brokered CDs (RT IV) are available in almost any currency you desire, generally with terms of six months to one year. These accounts are not insured by the FDIC. Also, because these are foreign accounts, they are subject to the withholding taxes of the foreign country.

Opening a Foreign Bank Account

Opening an account with a foreign bank may sound mysterious and complicated, but it is easily accomplished by mail, telephone, fax, or through the offices of a correspondent bank in the United States. Every country has its own banking laws, and the requirements for opening accounts will vary. Generally, a signature card is always needed and sometimes your signature must be notarized. Some countries require a copy of your passport to ensure that you are truly an alien, and therefore not subject to taxes paid by citizens. And, of course, an opening deposit must be made, with the minimum amount determined by the bank.

Before choosing an overseas bank, it is wise to ask about the tax policies of the bank's country. For example, Swiss banks are required to withhold 35 percent of the interest or dividends credited to your account. Because you do not need an account in a Swiss bank to hold an account denominated in Swiss francs, it makes more sense to open your account with a Netherlands or Luxembourg bank that has no withholding requirements. Although you can recover any money withheld by claiming a tax credit when you file your income tax form 1040, it is much easier to avoid the situation entirely when you choose your bank.

Once your account is opened, it can be used for many things other than buying CDs. If you desire to own a Swiss chalet, the advantages of having a Swiss bank handle the details will far outweigh the disadvantages of withholding on interest you receive. Should you wish to purchase stock in a Swiss company, again the bank can handle all of the details. These matters are discussed in more detail in Chapter 8.

Retrieving money from a foreign bank account is as easy as opening the account. You may request that a check in U.S. dollars be sent to you. This may take a couple of weeks and requires the additional step of endorsing and depositing the check into your U.S. bank account. A much faster way is to have your foreign bank wire funds to your domestic account. Tell your U.S. bank that you are due to receive funds from overseas. Ask for exact wire instructions from the bank, which you then fax to your overseas bank. Once these routing instructions have been received by the overseas bank, the transfer of funds can be made. The entire process should be accomplished within two or three days.

Most foreign banks will also provide you with a VISA or Euro-Card debit card that can be used worldwide at ATM machines. However, the currency you receive through the use of an ATM is the currency of the country in which the ATM is located, so if you are in France, you receive French francs. Only in the United States do you receive U.S. dollars from an ATM.

Foreign Banks That Offer CDs to United States Citizens

Services available from the following list of foreign banks vary according to the banking laws of the different countries. Some allow you to break the CD with only a small penalty, and others exact a very high penalty for early withdrawal. Some allow leverage on CDs, permitting you to own a $100,000 CD for $25,000 down and the rest a loan from the bank. Fees and interest rates also vary, with the highest rates and lowest fees going to the largest accounts. All these factors should be considered when opening an account.

Austria

Royal Trust Bank
Telephone: 43-1-43-61-61
Fax: 43-42-81-42
Mail: Rathaustrasse 20, P.O. Box 306, A-1011 Vienna
Minimum CD: $5,000 U.S.

Currency choices: Australia, Austria, Canada, France, Germany, Hong Kong, Japan, the Netherlands, New Zealand, Switzerland, United Kingdom, United States, and the ecu.

Denmark

Jyske Bank
Telephone: 45-31-21-22-22
Fax: 45-31-21-52-05
Mail: Private Banking International, Vesterbrogade 9, P.O. Box 298, DK-1501 Copenhagen V
Minimum CD: $15,000 U.S.
Currency choices: Australia, Canada, Denmark, Finland, Germany, the Netherlands, New Zealand, Norway, Spain, Sweden, Switzerland, United Kingdom, and the United States.

The Netherlands

ABN-AMRO
Telephone: 31-206-2827-64
Fax: 31-206-623-9940
Minimum CD: $15,000 U.S.
Currency choices: Australia, Austria, Belgium, Canada, Denmark, France, Finland, Germany, Greece, Hong Kong, Ireland, Italy, Japan, Malaysia, the Netherlands, New Zealand, Norway, Portugal, Singapore, Spain, Sweden, Switzerland, United Kingdom, United States, and the ecu.

Singapore

Hongkong Bank
Telephone: 65-530-5000
Fax: 65-225-01-663
Mail: 21 Coller Quay, Hongkong Bank Bldg., Singapore 0104
Minimum CD (Asian Currency Units, ACUs): $25,000 U.S.
Currency choices: All major currencies except (unbelievably)
Singapore dollars.

Switzerland

Overland Bank & Trust
Telephone: 41-1-482-6688
Fax: 41-1-482-2884
Mail: Bellariastrasse 82, CH-8038, Zurich
Minimum CD: $20,000 U.S.
Currency choices: Australia, Canada, Germany, Italy, Japan, the
Netherlands, New Zealand, Switzerland, United Kingdom,
United States, and the ecu.

Anker Bank
Telephone: 41-21-204-741
Fax: 41-21-239-767
Mail: 50, Avenue de la Gare, CH-1001, Lausanne
Minimum (Not CDs, but time loans to other banks are offered):
$5,000 U.S.
Currency choices: Australia, Canada, Germany, Italy, Japan, the
Netherlands, New Zealand, Switzerland, United Kingdom,
United States, and the ecu.

Answers to Questions You Might Forget to Ask

- No, foreign banks are not covered by FDIC insurance.
- Yes, you must report ownership of a foreign account on your IRS Form 1040.
- Yes, interest earned from overseas accounts is taxable in the United States.
- No, the overseas bank does not send a form 1099 reporting your earnings to the IRS. (This reporting requirement may be the chief reason so few U.S. banks are willing to offer foreign currency CDs. The expense entailed in adjusting computer software to encompass currency translations would be more costly than the bank's earnings from a limited number of accounts.)
- Yes, some countries tax your earnings by as much as 35 percent. This may be recovered as a tax credit when you file your U.S. tax forms. Better to open an account in a country without such withholding.
- Yes, money is quickly and easily credited to your local U.S. bank account at your direction. Although your overseas account may be in yen, pounds, or marks, your credits will be in U.S. dollars and you will pay for the exchange of the foreign currency into dollars.

◆ CHAPTER 8 ◆

Investing Directly in Foreign Securities

Diversification of investments through direct ownership of foreign securities is quite different from owning a portfolio of U.S. multinational companies. The pricing of foreign stocks is responsive to the general direction of markets in their own countries. Although those of western Europe tend to follow the U.S. market, those in other parts of the world often move in a contrary direction. A strong or weak dollar relative to the currency in which the company figures its gains and losses will have no effect on your investment until you receive dividends or the stock is sold.

Currency Considerations

Dividend payments to your account will be made in dollars unless you have an overseas account and have specified otherwise. If the dollar is strong at the time of exchange, your dividend will be decreased. Conversely, if the dollar is weak, you will receive a bonus of extra dollars from the exchange. The same formula applies when you sell your stock: Buy when the dollar is strong; sell when the dollar is weak.

American Depository Receipts

Until electronics made possible the transfer of stock ownership without certificates, it was difficult for U.S. citizens to trade foreign companies. An overseas agent had to be found to represent the buyer, not only to negotiate a price for the stock, but to arrange for its registration and transfer along with the necessary exchange of currencies. To this was added the time delay required to physically deliver certificates by ship from overseas. In 1927, J.P. Morgan invented American Depository Receipts (ADRs) whereby American banks would hold blocks of foreign securities and sell pieces to investors in the form of transferable receipts. Today, many of these ADRs (RT III) are listed on major American stock exchanges; approximately 10 percent of the issues listed on the New York Stock Exchange are foreign companies, traded as ADRs. These ADRs are traded in the same manner as stock issued by a U.S. company, that is, they are traded in dollars and transferred from seller to buyer through a U.S. transfer agent. Special reporting to the IRS is not required because you are not engaged in business with a foreign bank. However, because a tax of from 10 percent to 25 percent is deducted from your dividends at the source, you can recover this money only as a credit for taxes paid to a foreign government when you file your income taxes with the IRS.

ADRs are issued by a bank representing a block of foreign securities in its custody. American Depository Shares (ADSs) are similar, except that they are issued by a securities firm with the foreign securities in its custody. Global Depository Receipts (GDRs) are issued by several banks (some foreign) and may be traded on exchanges around the world. Depository receipts of all kinds are being issued at an accelerating rate with the increased privatization of European companies and the need to finance economic expansion in emerging third-world economies. To the purchaser, there is little difference among the types, other than the name. The term ADR has become generic and all variations serve the purpose of facilitating the investment in foreign securities. Even though a bank or securities firm may act as custodian for the underlying shares, that is the extent of its responsibility—there are no guarantees as to market performance. An important aspect of these securities is the number of ordinary shares represented by a single ADR. The number can vary from only a fractional share to multiple shares.

The development of electronic transfer has eliminated some of the original need for ADRs, but old habits die slowly. Investors have become comfortable having a bank act as an intermediary, and the banks are loath to forego the custodial fees charged for the service. Liquidity also is a factor in the continued viability of ADRs, which are often more easily traded than are the underlying shares.

Dividend Reinvestment Plans

Dividend reinvestment plans (DRIPs) (RT IV) represent a recent development in the markets for ADRs. DRIPs were an early feature of mutual funds that many U.S. corporations adopted as a means to enlarge the holdings of loyal shareholders. Although the mechanics of such plans served to exclude foreign companies, two ADR-sponsoring banks (Morgan Guaranty Trust and The Bank of New York) have instituted DRIPs for some of their ADR clients. These plans not only reinvest dividends, but allow the individual investor to make initial purchases of ADR shares, bypassing brokers. There are certain restrictions on minimum initial purchases and on additional cash purchases. In addition, initial enrollment fees and reinvestment service fees are charged. Withdrawal plans from both banks are also available for those that want monthly income checks. Withdrawal plans should be used only by those well versed in accounting. The frequency of buying and selling of the ADR shares complicates the establishment of a cost basis for each sale, and further complicates the filing for relief from foreign taxes on your IRS Form 1040.

Morgan Guaranty Trust Sponsored DRIPs

Morgan Guaranty Trust sponsors over 50 issues. Initial minimum purchase is $250 and an additional $15 enrollment fee is charged. Additional purchases may be made with a minimum of $50 and a maximum of $100,000 per year. Payments are invested on a weekly basis. A 5 percent fee to a maximum of $2.50 is charged for dividend reinvestment, and $5.00 plus 12 cents per share is charged for cash purchases. ADRs DRIPs sponsored by Morgan Guaranty may not be purchased by residents of North Dakota or Oregon. To find out more, call Morgan Guaranty Trust, Shareholder Services at 800-749-1687, or write to P.O. Box 8205, Boston, MA 02266-8205.

The Bank of New York Sponsored DRIPs

The Bank of New York sponsors 37 issues with DRIPs available. Their plans are similar to those of Morgan Guaranty Trust, but the fee structures are slightly different. Direct initial purchases are open to residents of all states. Initial purchases require a minimum of $200 and an enrollment fee of $10 is charged. Additional purchases are restricted to a minimum of $50 and a maximum of $250,000 per investment. Purchases are on a weekly basis as with Morgan Guaranty Trust. Each dividend reinvestment or cash purchase is charged a fee of $5.00 plus 10 cents per share. For additional information, call 800-943-9715, or write to Shareholder Relations Department, P.O. Box 11258, Church Street Station, New York, NY 10286-1258.

Today, many foreign companies are listing their shares directly on the major U.S. stock exchanges through the ADR route. This provides a simple way to raise capital in the U.S. market. Ordinary shares that are listed on a foreign exchange are usually identical to those traded in the country of origin, whereas an ADR may represent from a fraction to many ordinary shares. A foreign company that lists its ADRs on the New York Stock Exchange, American Stock Exchange, or Nasdaq must comply with the same Securities and Exchange Commission (SEC) reporting requirements as U.S. corporations. All expenses involved with meeting these requirements are borne by the company, along with the costs of exchange listing and distribution of dividends. Such ADRs are called "sponsored."

"Unsponsored" ADRs (RT V) result when the company does not seek listing in the United States, but merely acquiesces to the formation of ADRs for trading in the over-the-counter market. Buying unsponsored ADRs without a thorough investigation can present some real problems for the investor. These ADRs generally are not required to meet the SEC's reporting requirements and the investor must rely on sources other than the company for pertinent information. Additionally, the lack of reporting requirements may cause some state securities regulators to forbid the trading of these unsponsored ADRs in your state of residence. Even if your broker accepts your order and makes the trade, it may be rescinded at some future date, leaving you without the investment. You will be returned the money you paid, but your broker will pay for any loss or absorb any gain.

Pricing of many unsponsored ADRs presents an additional difficulty for the investor. Last week's prices may be taken from the "pink sheets" at your broker's office, but obtaining an up-to-the-minute quote entails the full cooperation of your broker's trading desk and you should expect to pay for this extra service in the form of commissions or expanded markups when a trade is executed. State securities regulators may present further difficulty by forbidding brokers to sell stock to residents of the state, if the companies have not received clearance by the state. These regulations were designed to protect residents of the state, so don't blame the broker who is unable to fill your order.

From the broad EAFE index (Europe, Australia, Far East) calculated by Morgan Stanley Capital International, nearly one-third of the approximately 1,000 international stocks comprising the index are traded in the form of sponsored ADRs. Given this broad availability of sponsored ADRs listed on the major U.S. markets, there seems little need for the average investor to "shop the pink sheets."

Appendix G provides a partial list of major foreign companies that are traded as ADRs in the United States. Many are global in their operations, so it is not wise to assume that their business results will exactly match the performance of the home country's economy. ADRs with dividend reinvestment plans are marked with the letters MGT or BNY to indicate sponsorship by Morgan Guaranty Trust or The Bank of New York, respectively. This list is an indication of the increasing availability of foreign companies to the U.S. investor. The appearance or nonappearance of any company on this list should not be taken as a recommendation to buy or sell that security.

Alternatives to ADRs

Should you desire to bypass the easy route offered by ADRs, two other means of obtaining ownership of foreign securities are available. You can open a foreign securities trading account (RT V) through any of several full-service brokerage firms (most discount brokers lack the facilities for international trading). You can also open accounts with the agents (often banks or government agencies) within each of the countries where the desired investments are headquartered. In either case, you can expect stiff financial requirements before your account is established. U.S. brokers ask for a deposit of $100,000 to $1 million before trading is permitted. Foreign securities firms, banks, and government agencies may impose equally stringent requirements. Transfer of securities and withdrawal of funds by foreign investors may be subject to government restrictions that can change overnight. Of course, ownership of foreign accounts also must be reported to the IRS.

Given the obvious advantages of ADRs, why do people bother with foreign accounts? The answer lies in the bond markets where few ADRs are available. The international bond market is enormous, with billions of dollars of trades every day. Do not look for a listing of government bonds from Albania, Zambia, or any country in between to be listed on the New York Stock Exchange. To enter this market on an individual basis, you need an international trading account.

The same general requirements to open an account with a foreign bank apply equally whether you wish to purchase, stocks, bonds, or CDs. You will find the procedure for opening your account at the end of Chapter 7.

Commonsense Investing Tips

- ADRs offer the simplest method of buying into foreign companies. Currency translations are avoided, and pricing is in U.S. dollars.
- Foreign banks will be happy to open an account for you and act as your broker in buying stocks on the local exchanges . . . for a fee!
- Taxes are withheld from dividends by the country in which the corporation is registered. Recovery of these taxes can be obtained when you file your U.S. income tax forms.

◆ FABLE ◆

The Lemming and the Vole

The vole had spent a busy morning gathering seeds and packing them away under the flat rock. Now he stretched out on the rock, feeling its warmth against his fat belly while the afternoon sun warmed his back from the tip of his nose to the end of his stubby little tail. His eyes slowly closed to the sight of the green meadow sloping gently toward the cliff overlooking the sea. He sighed contentedly and then drifted into sleep.

The vole was awakened by the excited cries of his cousin, the lemming. "Great news!" shouted the lemming as he bounded up the hill toward the flat rock. "We've been offered the opportunity of a lifetime! We'll be rich. No more work!" The words spilled out in such a torrent that it was hard to make any sense of them.

"Slow down," said the vole.

The lemming climbed up on the rock beside his cousin. "There will never be another chance like this one," he said. "A flock of ravens has offered to take our harvest of seeds to the lands across the seas where spring is just beginning. They will plant the seeds there and in a few months will harvest a hundred times as much."

The vole looked at his cousin with a questioning eye. "The ravens will do this out of kindness?" he asked, all the while wondering if ravens could be trusted.

"They'll take part of the seeds as payment for their trouble," the lemming answered. "They call it a commission."

"It sounds too good to be true. I think I'll pass," said the vole.

"It's the opportunity of a lifetime," repeated the lemming, "and everybody's doing it."

"Not quite everybody," the vole said, and closed his eyes to resume his nap.

The next day, all of the lemmings had gathered in the meadow between the flat rock and the edge of the cliff. They cheered wildly as one by one the ravens lifted the heavy sacks of seeds and flew off to the south. The vole shook his head in disbelief, then began again the task of filling the space beneath the rock with enough seeds to see him through the winter.

Summer passed, and the vole was atop the flat rock, thinking that it would soon be time to hibernate. He looked toward the edge of the cliff and beyond over the sea. In the distance there appeared a faint black shape, and the vole heard a cry from the meadow. "The raven is coming!" The cry was repeated, and soon the meadow seemed alive with lemmings, all shouting, "The raven is coming."

The raven landed in the midst of the lemmings. "Where is our grain?" the lemmings began to ask.

"There's so much, we couldn't carry it," the raven explained. "It has to come by ship."

"When? When?" the lemmings asked.

"Any time. You might even see the ship now if you go down to the edge of the cliff."

The lemmings needed nothing more. With glad cries of "Our ship has come in, our ship has come in," they swarmed down to the edge of the cliff. Their little furry bodies pressed against each other. Each one shoved and squeezed to get a better view of the sea beyond the cliff. Those in front, of course gave up looking. Instead, they scrambled to maintain their balance against the pressure of the horde.

Then, one by one, they began to tumble over the cliff until it seemed as though a brown waterfall of fur was plunging into the sea.

The vole sadly shook his head in disbelief. He would miss his cousin, the lemming. It was with a heavy heart that he crawled beneath the flat rock to begin his long winter sleep.

Moral: If you follow the crowd, your results will be the same as the crowd's.

◆

◆ CHAPTER 9 ◆

Investment and Speculation

Speculation Is Not a Dirty Word

Until now, we have been discussing areas that are generally considered to be investments; that is, the exchange of funds for selected assets from which we hope to obtain income. Buying an apartment building with the expectation of collecting rents from tenants would be an investment. Speculation may be defined as the placing of assets at risk in the expectation of increasing capital. Buying and rebuilding a dilapidated apartment building with the expectation of selling it for a price above its adjusted cost basis would be a speculation.

Consider the choice between an *investment* in a certificate of deposit (CD) for a stated return of 7.5 percent interest and the purchase of a nondividend paying stock as a *speculation* that the shares will increase in price. A good investment returns your capital with the expected interest: A good speculation increases your capital many fold. Had you invested $10,000 in a CD on January 2, 1996, you would have had $10,750 by January 2, 1997. In contrast, had you speculated with $10,000 in the American Depository Receipts (ADRs) of the little known Finnish firm Nokia, your account would have been worth $21,000 at the end of the same period. The definition bears repeating: Speculation is the placing of assets at risk with the expectation of increasing capital.

Speculation Is Not Gambling

Do not rush out and buy Nokia because it is mentioned here. That would not be speculation. It would be gambling! Speculation is often confused with gambling. Gambling relies entirely on chance. The probable results of a roll of the dice may be statistically supported, but the actual results of each roll depend entirely on chance. Speculation depends on predicting a future event through a careful weighing of known information. Judgment is the factor that differentiates speculation from gambling, and good judgment is the factor that differentiates successful speculation from failure.

The degree of speculation must be recognized before you put your money at risk. When buying stock in a company, is your decision based on reliable expectations of earnings or the potential for a new product? That would be classified as intelligent speculation. However, if your decision is based on the fuzzy feeling that in this "new era" all stocks must go up, or that price appreciation will follow "momentum," you are joining a crowd of gamblers. Adam Smith's *Popular Delusions and the Madness of Crowds* should be a basic textbook for any player in the world markets.

Whenever a whipping boy is needed to blame for some economic catastrophe, speculators are often characterized as the dastardly villains by the press and even government officials. When Thailand was forced to abandon a profligate banking and real estate binge in 1997, the government was quick to name the American financier, George Soros, as the speculator who toppled the baht.

Unfortunately, the role of speculative interests is little understood, even by Wall Street. Such terms as *market psychology, speculative excess,* and *herd psychology* are often used to describe a sudden change in markets. The act of labeling would seem to relieve the commentator of any need for thoughtful consideration of the relevant causative factors.

Speculators in currencies are often blamed for the excesses of governments that try to fix the currency exchange rates at levels that are divorced from reality. The ease with which currencies may be exchanged via wire connections today brings quick punishment to profligate governments, and makes the job of central banks much more difficult than in the past. The speculative forces of the world make governments correct fiscal abuses before the nations they govern become bankrupt.

Speculation Is the Magic of Wealth Creation

Speculators are often called parasites and accused of siphoning off unearned money from society while contributing nothing to the general welfare. Just the opposite is true. Where would the U.S. economy be today if Henry Ford had not risked his life savings along with those of his friends on the wild idea of an affordable car? How many jobs would not exist if Bill Gates had not speculated with his life savings in creating a new computer operating system? Indeed, 40 percent of the growth in the U.S. economy over the past five years may be directly attributable to high-tech industries that did not exist a decade ago. All this was created by people willing to speculate with their money, risking their futures on unproved ventures. Many of these speculators have become rich in the process, but society as a whole reaps far greater benefits.

Achieving wealth has never been easy. Interest on savings accounts can lead to a comfortable status over time, but wealth is gained primarily through speculation. The speculator weighs opportunity against risk. To dream of new products and processes has always been part of the American scene, but you do not have to be the dreamer, just recognize the potential of someone else's

FIGURE 9.1 The Investment Spectrum

RT V	RT II		RT I	RT III–IV	RT V
High	Low	←RISK→	Low	Moderate	High
Gambling	Saving		Investing	Speculation	Gambling
Not saving	Insured savings		AAA Bonds	Common stocks	Lottery

dream. The role of the speculator is to fund concepts and ideas without any guarantee of making a profit or even getting money back. To gather information and to use it in reaching an informed estimate of the future is hard work. To risk capital on the basis of a promising but unproved idea requires a strong character.

Speculation and investment are best viewed as a continuum, with no clear lines of demarcation. The person who hides his or her money beneath a mattress is speculating that the value of that money will remain constant over time. The person who deposits money in a savings account is speculating that the interest paid will exceed the rate of inflation and taxes. Likewise, the person who invests in blue chip stocks is speculating that their value over time will increase to a value greater than the sum of inflation and taxation. All decisions, even the decision to do nothing, must be based on some degree of speculation. (See Figure 9.1.)

The Choice Is Yours

Life is a series of choices. The worker has a choice between owning a fancy car or saving money for venture capital. The young couple may choose to have an immediate family before either partner is qualified for a high-paying job, or they may postpone having children until they complete their education and establish their careers. The choice is always between immediate gratification or the investment of time, energy, and savings toward long-term goals. The risk, of course, is that after a long period of deprivation, those long-term goals will not be realized. Capitalism does not guarantee success. However, the person who chooses to risk nothing in life has no right to complain about the wealth earned by successful speculators.

Accruing wealth through speculation is a long and sometimes stressful process. Not everyone is born with the emotional stability required to ride out the ups and downs of the markets while keeping long-term goals in mind. Fortunately, there are many levels of speculation open to everyone. One of the "Keys" in Chapter 10 will help you decide which level of speculation is most suitable for your emotional profile. Choose your comfort level and stick to it.

Two Elements in Building Wealth

Most people understand the value of compound interest to the investor. They sign up for dividend reinvestment plans to add shares to their mutual funds. They allow the interest on their savings accounts to be added to their principal, thereby gaining a larger interest payment in the following period. Yet the same people often look on speculative profits as an unexpected gift to be spent on some previously unaffordable luxury. Curiously, the idea that profits might be compounded is seldom considered. Spending profits is like cutting off the limb of a plum tree to harvest the fruit. Neither the tree nor the harvest will ever grow in size. Compounding profits is one of the essential elements in acquiring wealth.

Leveraging of assets is the second element of building wealth. The term *leverage,* like the term *speculation,* carries negative connotations for most people. Leverage, when applied to investments, means the borrowing of money to increase the size of your investment beyond the levels of your own capital. Most people employ leverage without knowing it when they buy a house. Down payments of 10–20 percent are common, with the remainder of the purchase price borrowed; for example, 80–90 percent on margin. Leverage produces a multiplier effect on investments. If you employ 50 percent margin (borrow money to pay for half of an investment), your potential for loss is increased by 100 percent and your potential profits will also be increased by 100 percent. Leverage increases both risk and rewards. You can buy U.S. Treasury bills with as little as 5 percent margin. Leverage in this case changes what many consider the safest of all investments into a very risky speculation. The amount of leverage available to you is determined by your broker, your bank, and the rules of an exchange. The actual amount of leverage you use is up to you, but a good rule for determining the amount is to never take a position that may require additional funds to maintain.

Although the compounding of profits and the leveraging of assets remain the cornerstones for building wealth, a third element should be added: concentration. Just as diversification is a major consideration in retaining wealth, concentration is an element in building wealth. To acquire wealth, you should concentrate your assets in those ventures that offer the best chance for success. "Pretty good" investments are offered every day, and they make up the bulk of the average portfolio. "Very good" investments must be sought out. Scattering your investments for the sake of diversification practically ensures that some of them will underperform the others. Cervantes cautioned, "'Tis the part of a wise man . . . not (to) venture all his eggs in one basket," but Mark Twain countered with, "Put all your eggs in the one basket and *watch that basket.*"

Speculation in currencies differs from other speculations only in its abstractions. When you buy bonds, stocks, or real estate, you have a tangible asset representing either debt or ownership. When you take a position in the currency market, you are making a reasoned choice between the relative future value of two economies as represented by their monies.

Tax Alert

In all of your ventures, you must keep in mind that you have a silent partner. The U.S. government is a full partner in all profits but a limited partner in losses. Although the government's cut of your profits has varied over the years at the whim of Congress, its participation in your net losses has remained fairly constant at $3,000. To avoid an unhappy surprise at tax time, it is a good idea to immediately set aside about 30 percent of all profits into a special account earmarked for the IRS. Or send this money to the IRS with your quarterly estimated tax. If you do this, you will not have to liquidate positions just to satisfy your need for cash when the taxes are due for the preceding year.

Commonsense Investing Tips

- Any venture that is undertaken with the expectation of increasing capital is speculative.
- The greater your knowledge of a venture, the less speculative it becomes.
- Never "go for broke." Ten percent of your investment capital should be the most you ever employ in purely speculative ventures.

◆ FABLE ◆

The Three Brothers' Bridges

Now, when one looks at that cement bridge that goes across the Snake River, it is hard to think about all the troubles those pioneers had when they came to this spot. Those who took this cutoff from the Oregon Trail hoped to save ten days, maybe two weeks, and the 60-mile trek north, even if the river was easier to ford up there. What they found here, stretching one-half mile on either side of the river, was rocky barrens. Not fit for farming, and the devil's own highway for wagons.

One of the earliest families to try the route was the Harrarts. Daniel Harrart was pressed into taking the shortcut because his wife was feeling poorly and was suffering cruelly from the jolting wagon. With his three boys tugging at the wheels, and the two oxen straining their hardest, he was able to get the wagon down to the river. It took two days, and the final lurch of the wagon twisted the left rear wheel between two boulders. The wagon was thrown on its side as the wheel fell apart.

Mrs. Harrart looked up from where she landed on the sandy river bank. "I think something broke," she said. "I don't think I can go on no more." She put down her head and seemed to go to sleep.

The next day, the three brothers helped bury their mother on a knoll above the high water mark left by the river. After the prayer, they heard their father say, "Boys, I've got to stay with your mother. I can't go on, even if we could fix the wagon."

For the next two weeks, they camped by the river, watching their father grow thinner. He didn't care about eating, and he'd quit shaving or washing. He just plain didn't seem to care about anything, just sat on the bluff and stared at the river. Like most teenagers, they soon gave up on him and spent their time fishing or skylarking in the river.

Some days along, they spotted a wagon coming down the rocky incline that had done them so much grief. For the next couple of days, they were busy helping move the wagon down the slope, being extra careful of the final drop onto the river bank. They near lost the wagon when she was caught by the current midstream, but they brought her steady with ropes slung to boulders on either side.

"Thanks for your help, boys," the man said. "We wouldn't have made it without you. It's worth $2 to me if you can help us up through that patch of rocks." The man spat a juicy mixture of tobacco and saliva toward the dubious passage.

"Done," said the oldest boy, and a day later they were back beside their overturned wagon, two-dollars richer. That night, the oldest boy laid out his plan. "Let's just stay here. We could earn a living from helping wagons make the crossing. We could even build a sort of rope bridge to make things easier." And that was the first bridge to go across the Snake River.

Things went pretty well for the next month or so. They helped seven more wagons across, and had $16 to show for it. The trouble came with the eighth wagon. The river had come up about a foot from rain in the mountains, and the rope bridge gave way. They picked up most of the wagon a mile down stream, but it took the better part of a week and most of their own wagon to put it right again. "We got to build a better bridge," the second brother suggested.

So, the oldest brother set out back to Fort Smith with $16 to buy a new wagon and lumber for a bridge. The trip took a couple of weeks, even though he hurried. But he was back in time to help bury his father who had given up and died of a broken heart. By now, winter was coming on, so they used some of the lumber to build a snug lean-to among the boulders. Hunting and fishing were good, so they didn't want for food.

Next spring, when the water went down some, they built the second bridge across the river, and set about to collect their tolls. Traffic was fair that summer, with about 20 wagons using the shortcut. But those rocks on either side of the river were a great discouragement. "You know," the youngest brother suggested, "If we was to make a proper road through them rocks, a lot more people would come."

"Too much work." The oldest brother scoffed.

"We're doing all right as we are," said the middle one.

"Well, I'm going to start and see what I can do," said the youngest.

"You know, we could just do the half leading down to the river. Once they get across the bridge, no one's going to want to go back."

And that's just what they did, only the youngest one insisted that they keep at it until the road stretched easy on both sides of the bridge. The road was so good, that over 100 wagons crossed the bridge the next year. The pioneers saved a full week or so of trekking and the three brothers became wealthy men.

The third bridge? That's the one you're looking at. Built in '35, I do believe.

Moral: Gambling takes courage; investment takes both courage and imagination; but speculation takes courage, imagination, and hard work.

CHAPTER 10

Speculating with Spot and Forward Markets, and Currency Options

So far, we have explored methods of placing assets in vehicles that are proxies for the exchange of dollars for foreign currencies. Each method has its peculiar benefits and drawbacks. Each must be carefully weighed against the probability of achieving the desired results. In this chapter, we will take the bold step of directly exchanging our dollars for another currency.

Fallen Angels

Disaster always attracts attention. It seems to be a natural law that the lion seeks the disabled for its prey, just as the pike will attack a wounded minnow. A shipwreck quickly attracts crowds of men bent on profiting from the salvage, just as the disastrous collapse of an economy elicits an instinctive thought that bargains have been created. Simple logic dictates that if a currency costs 20 percent less today than it did yesterday, then an easy profit can be had if the currency is bought and held until it regains its value. The problem is that the logic is too simple. Factors leading to the collapse of an economy can seldom be corrected overnight, and one might wait a lifetime for a currency to recover a previous valuation. As with most things in life, if a bargain seems too good to be true, it probably is no bargain. Caution is the watchword when approaching fallen angels.

Buying the Dips

You know that the maxim of profitable trading is "Buy low; sell high!" But you are cautious about the dangers of currency disasters. When, if ever, should you buy the fallen angels?

Currencies do not recover until the underlying economic reasons for the collapse have been corrected. Changing economic policies is very difficult for local politicians. It is much easier to blame external forces (such as currency speculators) than it is to eliminate nonproductive government spending. Although the collapse of a currency may be laid at the doorstep of domestic policies, the cure for the collapse usually requires the services of an outside doctor. The prescriptions of the International Monetary Fund (IMF) are often difficult to swallow, but they usually result in recovery if taken faithfully.

Thailand was crowned one of the tigers of Southeast Asia 1980s when its economy was growing at an astonishing 8–10 percent annual rate. When this rate slipped to a more usual 5–6 percent in 1996, the Thai baht showed signs of weakness against the U.S. dollar. Pegging the Thai baht to the dollar had been easy while the dollar was relatively weak against the Japanese yen. Funds from Japan flooded into Thailand, financing a boom in real estate that was financed by loans tied to the dollar. A strengthening of the dollar against the yen in 1996 made these dollar-pegged loans increasingly expensive to service, and inevitably affected the nation's foreign reserves. After more than a year of battling to hold the fixed baht-to-dollar rate in the face of declining reserves, the baht was freed from its dollar ties on July 2, 1997, and promptly fell by 15 percent.

The slowing economy, the overblown real estate market, and the dwindling of foreign reserves were all well known to the world markets before the final surrender of the baht to reality. The following weeks produced a further 10 percent slide of the baht. Moreover, doubts as to the valuation of other "tiger" currencies created turbulence in the regional currency markets. In late July, at the annual meeting of the Association of Southeast Asian Nations (ASEAN), Malaysia's prime minister Mahathir Mohamad epitomized political response to unpleasant economic turns by placing the blame on an international cast of villains, headed by the currency speculator George Soros.

While such rhetorical salve may have eased the political pain, it did nothing to cure the festering economic sore beneath. By December, the baht was worth less than 70 percent of its value six months before. A cure required the strong medicine provided by the IMF. The prescription called for elimination of the budget deficit through controlled spending and some increased taxes; the lifting of controls on capital flows that were imposed to squeeze foreign speculators; and the withdrawal of government financial support to insolvent companies, despite their political connections. Only when this prescription for recovery is fully accepted will the Thai baht offer a reasonable chance of gain for the investor.

Spot Markets

Whenever you cash a travelers check abroad, you have participated in a spot transaction. You have tendered U.S. dollars and received a foreign currency in exchange. On a scale millions of times larger, banks and corporations also make such transactions in what is known as the spot market. This is an arena for big boys with big bucks. Although the sums traded may be of any size, the standard minimum unit is $1 million. This is where central banks operate to smooth abrupt changes in the value of their currencies.

The Bank of England may sell a billion dollars to bolster the British pound, or the U.S. Treasury may sell 750 million British pounds to bolster the dollar. Creditworthiness is the major determinate of who is allowed to trade in these markets, and to determine to what extent a credit line is made available. Because the normal settlement date of a trade is two days following the trade date, a default on a trade is known almost immediately and will be reflected in the unwillingness of dealers throughout the system to ever trade with the delinquent party again. Where billions are traded on trust, trust becomes the ultimate currency.

Individuals may also exchange smaller sums through currency exchange windows in large city banks and international airports. This is not generally profitable: The spread between the buy and sell sides of such a transaction may be as much as two to three percent. To buy a few British pounds or German marks with the idea of later selling them at a profit would require a shift in the exchange rate of from 5 to 6 percent just to cover transaction costs. You are better off leaving the money in a savings account.

Forward Contracts (RT III)

A forward contract is an agreement to receive a specified amount of a certain good at a specific time in the future. You could say that a forward contract becomes a spot contract on the specified date. The chief advantage of forward contracts over spot contracts lies in this deferred settlement. The bank requires the deposit of full funds prior to settlement date for spot contracts, but generally requires a deposit of as little as 10 percent against a forward contract. However, additional funds may be required should your position deteriorate. Banks are able to offer such low margin requirements because they don't pay any funds to the seller until settlement day. Margin agreements usually entail the payment of funds to the seller when a transaction occurs. Payment is made with funds that have been lent by the bank or broker to the buyer, and the buyer must pay interest until the loan has been paid. Because no funds have been advanced to you, you pay no interest to the bank. Better yet, by locking in a fixed price for the foreign currency with a deposit of only 10 percent, you can invest the remaining 90 percent in U.S. Treasury bills that pay interest while you wait for the foreign currency to appreciate.

Because the settlement date for a trade is deferred to some future time, there is much less chance of a default. The individual investor is therefore allowed access to the forward markets in most currencies. If you desire a forward contract in a lesser known currency, such as the Myanmar (Burmese) kyat, you will be allowed less credit than you would for a contract in the Hong Kong dollar. The general rule is: The lower the trading volume of a currency, the higher the margin required to deposit.

In addition to a flexible margin requirement, the forward contract offers a flexible size. Some banks will write forward contracts for as little as $10,000 spot value of a currency. However, for a contract this small the bank will probably not offer any margin. Banks receive their income from fees and interest on loans, and there is very little of either for the bank writing small contracts.

The major drawback to using the forward contract is the timing element. Your forward contract is fixed in time, and a premature closing can be costly. It is unlikely that the bank can find a buyer for the exact size and remaining time of your contract. Should you be faced with the happy problem of locking in profits that came sooner than expected, you can buy an offsetting forward contract for the same size and settlement date as your profitable one. If your original forward contract was to buy 50,000 Hong Kong dollars at $1.25 U.S. and to settle 10 August, 1997, an offsetting contract would be to sell 50,000 Hong Kong dollars at $1.35 U.S. and to settle 10 August, 1997. Only the price of the Hong Kong dollar is different, reflecting the change that occurred since your original purchase. You will suffer additional fees for the new contract, additional margin, and *you will not have any funds available until settlement day.*

See Appendix H for a list of the currencies circulating within the regions and countries of the world.

Currency Options

The Scary World of Derivatives and Leverage

A derivative is any investment vehicle that derives its value from some other investment. Thus, an option has value only to the degree that value resides in the underlying asset. For example, if you have an option to buy an office building for $5 million, the value of the option would depend entirely on the value of the underlying real estate. If the building were appraised at $6 million, your option might reasonably be expected to be worth $1 million.

However, if real estate values dropped over the life of the option so that the building was appraised at only $4 million, your option would probably expire worthless. An option or futures contract like-wise derives its value from the cash value of the underlying asset, whether it be corn or currency. The prices of both options and futures will rise or fall based on expectations of price movements in the underlying assets. On both options and futures, premiums or discounts from intrinsic value will narrow as expiration or delivery dates approach.

Many horror tales about derivatives have been recorded by the press. The billion dollar loss by Proctor & Gamble and the bankruptcy of Orange County immediately come to mind. These stories emphasize the risk inherent in the *misuse* of derivatives. If you think of the derivative as an insurance policy whereby you can transfer an investment risk to a speculator, you will understand the true nature of derivatives. Just as you would think it foolish to act as an insurance company and guarantee to pay your neighbor the full value of his house should it burn down, so should you realize the folly of underwriting (selling) derivatives. In either case, the money you would receive in premiums would be insufficient to compensate you for the risk. True, it is unlikely that your neighbor's house will burn, but both Orange County and Proctor & Gamble thought it unlikely that interest rates could rise!

First, let us look at some of the basics of the options market for foreign currencies. An option is the right to either buy or sell a specific quantity of a currency at a fixed price within a specified time frame. Prices quoted for U.S. style options trades are always given in terms of U.S. dollars; for example, deutsche mark at $.5975, Swiss franc at $.6823. A *call* option provides the owner with the right to buy the specified currency for dollars. A *put* option gives the owner the right to sell the specified currency for dollars. For example, an option to *buy* 62,500 Swiss francs at $0.68 each, expiring in September, 1975, would be a call option. A put option would give the holder the right to sell 62,500 Swiss Francs at $0.68 each, expiring in September, 1995. Puts and calls are distinct types of options, and buying a call does not create a put on the part of the seller. The seller of an option merely creates a short position in the account for that option. Short positions may be offset by either delivery or buying in the shorted option.

Many options in other markets are settled by cash settlement, whereby the owner of the option receives a cash payment for the difference between the strike price and the settlement price at the time of expiration. Such is not the case for foreign currencies at present, although steps are being taken to allow for such settlement in the future. Currently, on exercised options, delivery is made in the country issuing the currency. This can result in considerable problems for the unaware trader. Foreign banking arrangements must be made, along with the payment of any taxes or fees imposed by that country. In addition, one must conform with U.S. regulations regarding the maintenance of a foreign bank account. It is much the wiser to close out currency options with offsetting transactions prior to expiration dates.

In summary, the buyer of an option has the right to exercise an option or to let it expire without exercising. The *total risk* exposure is the cost of the option. The seller of an option bears the risk and obligation to fulfill the contract if an option is exercised. In the case of selling a call option, the total risk exposure is unlimited unless hedged. In the case of selling a put option, the total risk exposure is limited to the total value of the underlying asset. In either case, the risks to the seller of an option are enormous in comparison to the amount of premium received. Therefore, to avoid the extra risks associated with the exercise of an option, restrict your actions to buying calls on a foreign currency when you think the dollar is weakening. Buy puts on the foreign currency when you think the dollar is strengthening. Be certain to close out either type of option by selling it prior to the exercise date.

Options on Foreign Currencies (RT IV)

Options on foreign currencies are similar to the forward markets, with two notable exceptions. First, the money paid for the option is not a down payment and is irretrievable. Second, the money paid for the option (premium) represents your total liability for the contract; you cannot be called for additional money if the position goes against you. All currency options contain two variables, the strike price and the expiration month. When you sell an option to close out a position, it is imperative that both of these variables match so that you do not inadvertently establish a straddle position. A third variable that might cause mischief to the unsuspecting option holder is the option style.

The style of European and American options differs as to when the holder of the option can exercise it. American options may be exercised any time before the expiration date. European options may be exercised only at the date of expiration. Therefore, the writer of an American option is at risk of exercise from the moment the option is created. The difference in the timing of exercise date between the two styles does not create a difference in the ability to trade and offset either style option throughout its life, although trading volume makes the American style more attractive in terms of liquidity.

Exchange Traded Options (RT IV)

Exchange traded options are standardized so that each option of a series is identical to all other options of that series as far as size, strike price, and duration of time. This standardization allows the exchange clearing house to stand as an intermediary on all trades. Thus, any option position may be liquidated without having to negotiate with the person who originally sold it. Options on foreign currencies are based on the same principles as listed equity (stock) options; that is, open positions after the last trading day are settled by physical delivery of the underlying asset. When an option in this market is exercised, delivery is made *in the country issuing the currency*. This stipulation can result in considerable problems not anticipated by the individual trader, such as conforming with U.S. and foreign regulations regarding the maintenance of foreign banking arrangements by U.S. residents. In addition, there may be taxes and fees assessed by the issuing country. With the exception of corporations that maintain foreign banking connections as a part of their business, most foreign currency options are closed out with offsetting transactions prior to the expiration dates. The Exchange is currently in the process of designing a system for cash settlement in place of delivery, but implementation is still in the future.

The Seller Bears the Risk

Remember, the buyer of the option has the right to exercise and the seller bears the risk and obligation to fulfill the contract. Therefore, if you wish to avoid the extra risks associated with an exercised option, restrict your actions to buying calls on a foreign currency when you think the dollar is weakening and to buying puts when you think the dollar is strengthening. Just be sure to sell the option prior to the last trading day.

Intervention

Since 1971, when the Bretton Woods agreement for fixed exchange rates was abandoned, the relative value of the U.S. dollar to other major currencies has been permitted to fluctuate. The extent of the fluctuation has, from time to time, been limited by actions taken by the various governments. The possibility of intervention by a central bank, including the U.S. Federal Reserve, or the imposition of restrictions to the movement of currencies across borders adds a special risk to foreign currency trading. This extraordinary risk, unique to currency trading, underlines the advantage of being an option buyer, whose maximum risk is the cost of the option.

Most foreign currency transactions occurring in the interbank market involve sums that are substantially larger than the amounts called for by a single option. These transactions are not recorded by any central reporting system; therefore, while the quotation information available from your broker or newspaper is fairly accurate, it should not be taken as a precise reflection of the current spot market.

Determining Trends

Earlier, we suggested that a chart of weekly closes would be sufficient for determining the long-term trend of a currency in relation to the U.S. dollar. Now that we are considering highly leveraged positions, where even short-term trends can produce sizable gains or losses as a percentage of the capital employed, the weekly chart will no longer suffice. The simplest means of determining when a short-term trend is changing is to employ a daily-close chart as an overlay to the weekly chart.

FIGURE 10.1 Weekly Closes

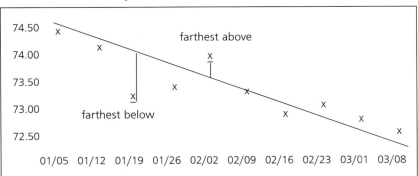

First mark in the weekly closes for the preceding 20 weeks, allowing five spaces between each mark. Next, use a ruler to add a line so that the weekly marks cluster above and below the line. You will note that the resulting straight line is trending either up, down, or straight across. This is the long-term trendline. Extend it to the edge of your graph paper to give a projected trendline. Next, mark the daily closing prices in each of the spaces between the weekly marks, continuing over the projected trendline. These daily-closing marks generally fall near the projected trendline. Only when the daily marks are a significant distance from the projected trendline is a change of trend indicated.

What distance is significant? Go back to the first weekly close and then trace along the long-term trendline until you find the weekly close that is farthest above or below the trendline. Any succession of three or more daily closes greater than this distance from the trendline should be considered a significant change in direction for the short to intermediate trend. While this method is simple to the extreme, it has been found to be reasonably reliable over the years. (See Figure 10.1.)

If you find the task of charting too tedious, a subscription to a charting service offers considerable relief. An excellent service is provided by the Commodity Trend Service. Call them at 800-331-

1069 to find the charts that are best suited to your purpose and the subscription cost, or write to them at Commodity Trend Service, P.O. Box 32309, Palm Beach, FL 33420.

Foreign Currency Option Specifications (Philadelphia Options Exchange)

The regular expiration cycle of March, June, September, and December applies to all of the currencies. These months are continuously listed; for example, when March of current year expires, March of next year will be listed. All Philadelphia Exchange Options define the day of expiration as the Saturday *preceding* the *third Wednesday* of the expiration month. The last time you may trade an option is, therefore, 1:30 PM Eastern Time (U.S.) on the business day immediately preceding the expiration day. Trading hours on the currencies are from 8:30 AM to 2:30 PM Eastern Time (U.S.).

Figure 10.2 gives you some additional information pertinent to each currency. Remember, to find the value of an option, you must multiply the quoted price by the amount of currency in the contract. For example, if an option quote on the British pound is 1.12 cents, and the size of contract is 31,250, then the price of the option is $350.

Cross Rate Options

If you think that two currencies will change in value relative to each other but not relative to the U.S. dollar, then consider cross rate options. These options permit you to be long in one foreign currency and short in another with a single option. For instance, if you think that the German mark will strengthen in relationship to the Japanese yen, then you would want to own a call option on the German mark/Japanese yen Cross. If you think that the Japanese yen will be the stronger currency, then you would want to own a put

FIGURE 10.2 Contract Specifications
(Philadelphia Options Exchange)

Currency	Ticker Symbol	Contract Size	Quote Intervals	Strike Intervals
British pound	XBP	31,250 pounds	1 U.S. cent	1 U.S. cent
Canadian dollar	XCD	50,000 dollars	1 U.S. cent	2 U.S. cents
French franc	XFF	250,000 francs	.1 U.S. cent	.25 U.S. cent
German mark	XDM	62,500 marks	1 U.S. cent	.5 U.S. cent
Japanese yen	XJY	6,250,000 yen	.01 U.S. cent	1 U.S. cent
Swiss franc	XSF	62,500 francs	1 U.S. cent	.5 U.S. cent

option on the German mark/Japanese yen Cross. Standardized pricing of these options uses the quantity of the smaller contract as the multiplier (in this case the German mark). Options on cross rates are seldom traded, so liquidity is curtailed.

◆ FABLE ◆

Marlow T. Humphrey was rich. He drove a Rolls Royce from his mansion in Hillsborough to his broker's office each day, but he had little time for the regulars who gathered to watch the tape. He conducted his business like a patron in a four-star restaurant: He ordered and the broker dutifully provided. Today he was particularly meticulous with his instructions.

"Sell four contracts of March British pounds, at the market."

The broker was surprised. "You'll need a commodity account for that."

"Details, always details. Give me the papers to sign and you can fill in the details later. You should have all the information from my other accounts."

The broker was reluctant. "Have you ever traded commodities before?"

"I don't know why I'm explaining," Marlow said with a touch of irritation. "I've just returned from a world affairs seminar, and the thought is that the new Thatcher Government in England is bound to fail. I may not entirely agree, but sometimes one needs to defer to expert opinion. Now, please sell those British pounds for me." The deal was done, and Marlow left the office committed to deliver 100,000 British pounds in March of the following year.

During the next week, the Thatcher Government gained strength, taking the British pound with it. Marlow was $15,000 in the hole when he decided to double his position by selling another four contracts. That meant that the pound would have to drop only one-half of its recent rise to make him even. Such determination was not lost on the broker. Marlow must really know something. Even a rich man wouldn't commit an additional exposure of $100,000 without some assurance of success.

The broker did some quick calculations of his own finances, and concluded that he could swing one contract if he margined all of his stock account. He wrote a ticket to sell one March British pound contract for his own account, debated momentarily about the ethics of riding the coattails of his wealthy client, then handed the order to the wire operator. By the end of the day, he had lost $300 when the pound closed at the trading limit. He barely slept that night.

In the following three days, the broker grew haggard from sleepless nights. As the British pound crept relentlessly upward, he was forced to borrow on his credit cards to meet a call for more margin. Marlow seemed totally unconcerned during this time of mounting losses; his margin calls were easily met by the automatic transfer of funds from his other accounts. Only after the pound had climbed an amazing 35 cents against the dollar did Marlow seem to take notice.

"So much for experts," he exclaimed. "Buy eight March British pounds at the market."

The broker's hand shook as he wrote the order. The pound was still advancing, and it was impossible to immediately liquidate his own position without revealing that he had been riding on Marlow's coattails. The few moments it took to receive a report of execution on Marlow's order seemed as long as the previous sleepless night. At last it came. "Looks like you lost a lot of money," the broker said, trying to hide the anxiety in his voice.

"No," Marlow replied, "that was just a partial hedge against my forward contract at the bank. I have a half-million stake there, and that seminar made me worry a bit. The hedge let me sleep nights."

The broker watched Marlow T. Humphrey climb into his Rolls Royce. He stood dumbfounded as the car drove off, leaving him so shaken that he almost forgot to cover his own position.

Moral: A little knowledge can be a dangerous thing, especially if you are playing follow the leader.

◆ CHAPTER 11 ◆

Speculating with Futures and Options on Futures

The Basics

Currency futures (RT V) are traded on a commodity market, the International Monetary Market (IMM), a subdivision of the Chicago Mercantile Exchange. On this exchange, currencies are bought and sold in the same manner as wheat, pork bellies, and crude oil. Like other commodities, prices are quoted in terms of the U.S. dollar. A bushel of wheat might sell for $4 a bushel, pork bellies may sell for $.97 per pound, and a barrel of crude oil could sell for $22.35. Like-wise, a British pound may be quoted as $2.75, while a German mark might be $.59. To determine the total value of the commodity traded, the unit price must be multiplied by the contract size. A contract of wheat represents 5,000 bushels, so if the unit price is $4 the total contract would have a $20,000 value. The German mark trades in units of 125,000 so, at $.59 for each mark, the total contract would equal $76,700.

Standardization

Remember that forward contracts may be of any size that suits the needs of the buyer. A futures contract is an agreement between two parties, a buyer and a seller, for a specific standardized quantity of a given asset. All contracts for each currency are of an identical size; for example, all deutsche mark contracts are for exactly 125,000 German marks. The liquidity of futures trading is dependent on the interchangability of the contracts, a liquidity not available on the forward markets. The futures trader is able to take profits or cut losses through offsetting orders without the delays inherent in liquidating a forward contract.

Futures contracts, unlike options, have no strike price. The price at which you enter the market either as a seller or a buyer becomes the benchmark against which profit or loss is determined. With options, you paid a premium when buying either a put or call, and you received a premium when the option was sold. The difference between the premium paid on the purchase and the premium received on the sale represented your profit or loss. Unlike option trades, no money is paid to the seller by the buyer of a futures contract. Instead, both the seller and the buyer must deposit a sum ("margin") that serves as good faith money to ensure fulfillment of the contract by both parties. Although this deposit is called initial margin, it remains your money and is shown as a credit to your account. As with forward contracts, you have not borrowed any funds from the broker, so there are no interest charges to pay.

The key point to remember is that in a futures contract both parties have assumed an obligation: the seller to deliver, and the buyer to receive delivery of the asset. It is the seller who determines the exact date of delivery (within the specified delivery period), and only when delivery is made will full payment exchange hands. Prior to delivery, either party may cancel the obligation by making offsetting transactions in the futures market (the buyer must sell an identical contract; the seller must buy an identical contract). The liquidation by only one party does not cancel the contract held by the other party. A new party has assumed the liquidated position. When an offsetting transaction is made, the difference between the initial contract price and the liquidation price will yield either a gain or a loss to the trader.

How the System Works

Liquidation by way of offsetting transactions is the most frequent method of settling futures contracts. Actual delivery accounts for only about 3 percent of all contracts traded. The Exchange Clearing Corporation makes the system work. It acts as a third party in every transaction, representing the buyer to every seller and the seller to every buyer. A secondary function of the clearing corporation is to ensure the financial integrity of every futures contract. This is accomplished by requiring daily cash settlements. At the close of every trading day, the closing price of each position is compared to the previous day's closing price. The clearing corporation then calculates the gain or loss and debits or credits the brokerage firm that is the nominal holder of the position.

Margin Calls

Should a customer's account be reduced below the minimum requirements by this "mark to market," the customer will be called on for additional margin. Calls for additional margin are triggered when the equity in your account falls below initial margin requirements by 25 percent. Initial margin deposited by both parties is only a small percentage of the total value of a contract (usually about 10 percent), so a change of only 2.5 percent of the contract value could result in a margin call. Should a market move sharply in a direction opposite to that expected, the holder could lose the entire initial deposit, and be called for even more. Margin calls can be satisfied through liquidation of positions rather than the deposit of new money, unless your account is in deficit. This is generally the best course to follow with a losing position.

On the other hand, because every contract consists of two sides, those margin calls on one side become credits to the other side. Excess margin credited to a customer's account may be withdrawn without closing out the position. It may also be used as initial margin to increase your positions. The ability to withdraw profits without liquidating a position is one of the major attractions of the futures markets.

Tracking a Trade

The following example tracks a typical currency futures trade and shows each of the preceding points.

Assumption

Assume that you think the dollar will decline against the German mark.

What You See

You find that the current spot price is $.5906.

What You Do

You buy one contract of December deutsche marks at $.59870

What You Get

The first thing you will notice is that you paid a higher price for delivery in December than you would have paid for immediate delivery. This is a "carrying cost" differential representing lost interest income and an assessment of the seller about the future course of the German economy.

Your confirmation from your broker will show that you have a contract to receive 125,000 German marks on any business day after December 1st (the exact day is at the discretion of the seller), for which you are obligated to pay $74,837.50 plus commission and delivery fees. The actual delivery will be made in a bank in Germany, and it is up to you to make any arrangements for personal delivery to you.

Your broker will require a margin deposit on the day of the trade (usually before your order is entered). In this case, assume that he requires $5,000 as initial margin. Commission costs will be charged when the position is closed by either offsetting or delivery.

Your account will look something like this:

Initial cash (margin)		$ 5,000.00 CR
Position	Long 1 IMM DMK Dec. @ .59870	$74,837.50
Market price	$.59870	$74,837.50
Market variation		$ 0.00
Equity		$ 5,000.00 CR

If the deutsche mark should rise by $.0037 to $.60240, you would see:

Initial cash (margin)		$ 5,000.00 CR
Position	Long 1 IMM DMK Dec. @ .59870	$74,837.50
Market price	$.60240	$75,300.00
Market variation		$ 462.50 CR
Equity		$ 5,462.50 CR

Should you elect to withdraw $400, your account would then read:

Initial cash (margin)		$ 5,000.00 CR
Withdraw cash		$ 400.00 DB
Cash (margin)		$ 4,600.00 CR
Position	Long 1 IMM DMK Dec. @ .59870	$ 7,483.50
Market price	$.60240	$75,300.00
Market variation		$ 462.50 CR
Equity		$ 5,062.50 CR

Now, suppose a few days later, the mark drops by $.0079 to $.59450.

Cash (margin)		$ 4,600.00 CR
Position	Long 1 IMM DMK Dec. @ .59870	$74,837.50
Market price	$.59450	$74,312.50
Market variation		$ 525.00 DB
Equity		$ 4,075.00 CR

You are now dangerously close to a margin call. If your equity had dropped to $3,750 or below, you would be called to deposit enough money to bring your equity back to $5,000. Because each $.00010 (from 0.59750 to 0.59760) equals $12.50 per contract, a further drop of only .00260 to 0.59190 will trigger a call.

Suppose you did nothing and the mark dropped to $.59170:

Cash		$ 4,600.00 CR
Position	Long 1 IMM DMK Dec. @ .59870	$74,837.50
Market price	$.59170	$73,962.50
Market variation		$ 875.00 DB
Equity		$ 3,725.00 CR
Margin required		$ 5,000.00
Margin call		$ 1,275.00

Thus, you would have to return the $400 withdrawal plus an additional $875 to maintain your position. Had you not made that initial withdrawal, there would have been no call. Sometimes a little excess margin provides room to breathe.

Rather than meeting the call for $1,275, suppose you liquidate the position:

Cash (margin)		$ 4,600.00 CR
Position, Purchase	Long 1 IMM DMK Dec. @ .59870	$74,837.50
Position Sold	Short 1 IMM DMK Dec. @ .59170	$73,962.50
Difference		$ 875.00 DB
Adjusted cash		$ 3,725.00 CR

The loss of $875 on an investment of $5,000 equaling 17.5 percent seems extraordinary for such a short time, and it would be prohibitive if it were true. What must be considered in assessing the results is the erroneous thought that your investment was $5,000. Your investment was $74,837.50 even though you were required to deposit only $5,000. Your percentage loss was actually barely over 1 percent. To gain perspective, put the trade in terms of the stock market. Say that you bought 1,000 shares of a stock at 74⅞. A few days later, the stock dropped to 74 and you sold the 1,000 shares for a loss of $875. Although such a stock trade would require a deposit of about $37,500, the profit or loss would be figured in relation to the investment, not the margin requirement.

If you are able to think in terms of the total value of your investment, rather than in terms of the margin required, you will be much better equipped to ride out the minor fluctuations in price. Study the market well before you invest. Keep excess margin money immediately available in a money market account. Place your funds with caution and sell reluctantly. Remember, trends in currencies last for years, not days.

The Ultimate Option

An option on a futures contract (RT V) compounds the leverage of the futures markets with the leverage of options. Despite this feature, an option on a futures contract is really no more complicated or hazardous than the options previously discussed. For the buyer, the risk is limited to the cost of the option. It is the seller (writer) of the option who assumes an indeterminate risk in exchange for the premium received. Most sellers of options write against futures contracts they own, thereby limiting their risk to only a loss of profit potential beyond the money received from the option sale.

When a currency futures option is exercised, the holder of the option receives a position in the futures market, not the delivery of currencies. This position in the futures market will be a long position if a call option is exercised or a short position if a put option is exercised. When exercising an option on the futures, you assume all of the obligations of the futures market as to initial and maintenance margins. It is the buyer (holder) of an option, and only the buyer, who has the right, but not the obligation, to exercise the option.

Avoiding Confusion

The seller (writer) of the option receives the premium paid by the buyer and is obligated to take an opposite futures position when and if the option is exercised. In order to deliver a long position when a call option is exercised, the writer must assume a short position in his own account if he does not already have a long position to deliver. Likewise, a writer of a put option must already have a short position to deliver from his account or be prepared to assume a long position versus the delivery. Often a writer of an option employs stop orders that allow him to write "naked" options. A "naked" option is one that is not covered by an existing deliverable position. The stop order will be placed at a level where it will be executed before there is any likelihood that the option might be exercised. The premiums charged for options are often in excess of the margin requirements for the position, so the writer uses the premium money to cover the offsetting position—about as close to a free ride as you will ever find.

Options on currency futures usually expire two Fridays before the third Wednesday of the contract month. The last day of trading for the futures contracts is usually the second business day immediately preceding the third Wednesday of the contract month. This allows the person exercising an option about two weeks to decide how to dispose of the futures contract. Because these dates are subject to changes under certain circumstances, it is best to consult with your broker prior to entering the markets.

Commonsense Investing Tips

- Margin requirements are extremely low in relation to the total value of the contracts traded in futures markets. The tendency to become overextended may be countered by using U.S. Treasury bills as collateral, never using more than 20 percent of the Treasury bill value for commodities trading.
- Short-term moves are often sharp and erratic and should be ignored. Do not try to outguess them. Stick with the long-term trend.
- As your profits mount, withdraw them to employ in less volatile markets.

◆ FABLE ◆

A Board Room Game

Charlie knew the kind of trader he was. "I don't have enough sense to go against my own better judgment," had become his watchword. He was a flipper, buying corn one day and shorting pork bellies the next, trading one position for the other, each time with the certainty that what he held from the previous day had become worthless overnight. "Get me out," he would scream, "I can't stand another loss."

Of course, we all knew that he could afford it. He was relatively well off for an old man. No, it wasn't the losses, rather it was the principle of the thing. Each time he made a trade, he placed his ego on the line before the other traders who watched the whizzing tapes. There was a craving within his soul to show the world that he was a spectacular money maker.

"Now, there's a man with both feet planted firmly in midair," John remarked with a scornful glance toward Charlie. John had inherited a bit of midwest land that was farmed on a share-crop basis; so he fancied himself to be a gentleman farmer and therefore a shrewd speculator. "You have to stick with it, Charlie, if you want to make any money." Although his words were addressed to Charlie, he spoke loudly enough for all to hear, and even swung his head to face the others so as to enjoy their approving looks over his wise pronouncement.

"I don't notice you making so much money," Charlie muttered before he turned back to the broker. "Have you got those orders in?"

"Yes, you're selling 2 July copper at the market and buying two contracts of December Swiss francs at the market."

John seemed caught in a spasm. "Swiss francs? What a plunger! You don't know anything about Swiss francs."

Charlie gave John a disdainful look. "I've been to Europe," he said. Then he turned to the broker. "Treasury Secretary Blumenthal has been on TV every night explaining how he's going to solve the balance of payments by making the dollar weak. That's supposed to make our exports cheap so foreigners will buy more."

"You don't believe him?"

"Do you think the Germans are going to buy Chevies instead of Volkswagens just because the price of a Chevy drops a few hundred marks?"

"Probably not."

John had been impatiently waiting for a chance to break in. "That's unpatriotic, you going against the dollar."

"Unpatriotic?" Charlie was really getting peeved. "If the government wants a cheap dollar, it would be unpatriotic *not to help.*" He twisted back to the broker. "What I do is my own business. From now on, I don't want anyone to know what positions I take. Understood?"

The broker backed away, but when he returned with the reports on Charlie's orders, he kept his voice so low you could barely hear it. "You lost $50 plus commissions on the copper, and you bought two Swiss at $.3914."

Charlie checked the quote machine. The Swiss franc showed 3912. He had a loss of another $50. His jaw tightened. "Just don't tell that son of a bitch anything!"

The Swiss franc closed at 3927, giving Charlie an unrealized profit of 13 points—$325 for the two contracts. He left the office with the air of a man who had just won the Irish Sweepstakes. In the following days, the Swiss franc showed a definite upward trend, reaching 3983 before making a sudden downward plunge to 3937 in a single trading session. That day he saw his profits evaporate by $1,150 to a modest $575. Unfazed, Charlie maintained his equanimity throughout the ordeal, but now, even while seated, his foot danced whenever he crossed his legs. It was only when the Swiss franc cleared 4000 that he showed signs of relaxing, even to the point of saying good morning to John.

Hubris is endemic to humanity and Charlie was no exception. In June, the Swiss franc spurted to 4467 and Charlie's account showed an equity of $20,825—mostly the unrealized profits of $13,825. He had quietly tripled his initial margin deposit in less than four months. On the 23rd of June, Charlie proclaimed victory over the markets and John.

It should have been a tableau of great drama, had John not been engrossed in conversation with the man next to him. Charlie stood, looking impatiently at John, then spoke in a voice much too loud to be ignored. He commanded the broker, "Buy two more December Swiss at the market."

That caught John's attention. He stiffened his back and pulled in his gut as much as he could. "Some people just don't have any respect for their country," he accused. "We're struggling overseas and you're selling the dollar short!"

"No more unpatriotic than selling corn short, and a whole lot more profitable." Charlie was now smirking. Corn had moved up about ten cents in the previous week, and he knew that John was stubbornly holding a short position. "I've made over $10,000 in the Swiss already. Actually, it's closer to $13,000, but I didn't want it to seem like I was bragging."

John, for once, seemed at a loss for words. "Of course not," he muttered.

That night the news carried the story of over $30 billion Treasury bills purchased by foreign accounts in 1997 alone. Robert Solomon, Treasury Under-Secretary for International Affairs, blithely commented, "We are financing the deficit through a fully autonomous net inflow of foreign capital." Whatever the intent of his comment, the dollar stabilized the next day, then moved a hundred points higher against the Swiss franc during the following week. Now that he had four contracts, each point was worth $50 to Charlie. He saw the profit on his original contracts rapidly dwindle, while the losses on his added positions multiplied. The strain began to show in his eyes. They became glossed over with a reddish tint. He had not slept well for days.

John realized that Charlie was again a vulnerable target and was unrelenting in his taunting. "Better sell out while you have something left. It doesn't pay to bet against the United States Treasury unless you have more money than God."

Charlie could only sit and squirm in the misery of indecision. What if John was right? What if he lost all of his profit. What if he lost all of his money? The market was down again, bringing him ever closer to the horrible point where additional margin was required. By midday he broke. He told the broker, "Sell two December Swiss."

The executed order was at 4338. Charlie had sold his initial contracts for a profit of $10,600, but his unrealized loss on the second commitment he still held had reached $5,750. His total equity was now $12,200. As he did the calculations, a thin line of perspiration formed on his upper lip and his leg began its dance.

Mechanically, he checked the monitor on the quote machine watching each mocking tick. Suddenly he stiffened. "I knew it," he shouted, no longer trying to hide his anguish. "They were waiting for me to sell out!" His voice dropped to a drawn-out sob, "Look, they're running the Swiss back up." The monitor showed the Swiss franc at 4351, 13 points higher from where he had sold. Charlie slumped back and fumbled a handkerchief free of his jacket to wipe the sweat for his face. It left tracks of reddened skin across his cheeks and forehead. Between short gasps for breath, he managed to give the broker another order. "Buy 'em back!"

The broker looked astonished. "What?"

"Buy them back. At the market, right now."

"You'll need more money. There isn't enough left in your account to carry four contracts."

"I'll bring it in tomorrow, just get those contracts back."

The Swiss franc closed at 4372, justifying Charlie's judgment, but making a shambles of normal accounting. His in-and-out trading meant that he had not liquidated his original contracts. His account would show only a day-trade of two contracts for a realized loss of 17 points, only $425, and he would still be long four contracts at their original costs. The terrible draw-down of equity would not show on a realized profit and loss statement, but could still trigger a margin call.

The angels were truly watching over idiots that day. Despite the realized loss on the day-trade, Charlie's repurchase of the two contracts, aided by a higher closing, had restored enough equity in his account to forestall the need for more money.

The next morning Charlie looked pale when he came in. He must have been expecting the worst. He shuffled across the floor to the quote machine and lowered himself heavily beside the broker.

"Bad night, Charlie?"

"No, just a little dizzy spell when I got out of the car. Left me sort of weak, but it'll pass." Charlie settled into the chair for a moment before he asked, "What do I owe?"

"You're in the clear, no call," the broker said. The broker smiled at the bewildered look in Charlie's eyes, and he hurried to explain. "When you sold, that reduced your exposure to only two contracts, so your maximum exposure was for only four contracts during the day. Had you bought first, that would have increased your exposure to six contracts and you would have had a margin call for the extra two as a day-trade."

Through the summer, the dollar continued to weaken while the stock market soared. Foreign investors were using the excess dollars created by the trade deficit to buy into U.S. companies. German, Swiss, and even British citizens were receiving the equivalent of a 10 percent discount when their money was exchanged for dollars in the U.S. markets. A report from a congressional subcommittee placed a sanguine glow on the most recent trade reports:

> Dollar depreciation and modest wage increases have
> encouraged foreign investors to establish manufacturing
> operations within the United States. . . . These benefits

should not be overlooked, and so long as they result from the workings of economic forces in exchange markets rather than government manipulation, we should feel no embarrassment about enjoying them.

Charlie enjoyed himself immensely as the dollar plummeted and his equity soared. The exchange increased margin requirements on the Swiss franc from $3,500 to $5,000 per contract in October to dampen speculation, but by then it was trading over 4600. Charlie's average cost basis on the four contracts was 4184. At $50 per point, he was ahead by $20,800 and could easily carry his positions, even with a 40 percent margin increase. He sat and watched the monitor with the intensity of a cat at a mousehole.

By mid-November, Charlie's contracts broke above 5000, doubling his unrealized profits again. He was becoming noticeably edgy as the first notice day approached. Prior to delivery day, it would be necessary for him to sell out. If he held for delivery, he would have to open a bank account in Switzerland and deposit $209,200 to pay for the 500,000 Swiss francs stipulated in his contracts. Charlie didn't want to get off the gravy train, but there was no way he could meet those requirements.

Day after day, he twisted nervously in his seat, the foot at the end of his crossed leg twitching as though keeping time to a syncopated drum beat. "Should I sell out now?" he would ask, and the monitor would click another point or two of profit as the Swiss franc continued up. "No," he would answer himself, "let's wait a little longer." Then a down-tick or two and he would ask again, "Should I sell out now?"

Finally, external events forced a decision. The heads of the central banks of Europe and Japan announced a meeting, to be held in Paris on December 8, to agree on a concerted effort to stem the fall of the dollar. The Swiss franc immediately dropped seventy points and Charlie sold out at 4971. After paying $400 in commissions and an exchange fee of $4, Charlie netted $38,946.

He took a check for the full amount in his account and announced that he was taking his wife to Acapulco for the holidays. This grand gesture brought a look of envy to John's face, which Charlie graciously overlooked. While he was gone, Secretary of Treasury Blumenthal absolutely refused to take part in the effort of the other central banks to support the dollar. By December 20th, the Swiss had gained an additional 200 points. Charlie had left $10,000 on the table, but how can you put a price on peace of mind? Charlie enjoyed his sojourn in Mexico.

Moral: You can't win it all, so take time to enjoy what you do win.

Note: Before the advent and proliferation of electronic quotation machines in the 1980s, brokerage offices were arranged like theaters. The ticker tape that displayed prices was projected onto a screen at center stage and customers were provided comfortable seats from which they could view the show. The atmosphere of a club prevailed among regular customers.

The 10 Keys to Successful Global Investing

1. Know Yourself

Think of yourself as the chief executive officer (CEO) of a corporation that is your single, most important resource—your life. You must decide what health care measures to take, what education you need, and what long-term goals are within your abilities to achieve. To be successful, any business must be intelligently directed along a well conceived path called a business plan, yet millions of people stumble through life without any sort of plan.

Your temperament largely determines the sort of plan you should make. Take the time now to seriously consider all aspects of your life, not just your financial goals. Financial success is only useful when it facilitates reaching other, more important, goals. Money will not, of itself, ensure for a happy home, self-reliant children, lasting friendships, or the respect of those you love. It can, however, provide the leisure time needed to improve your golf game, learn a foreign language, travel, or write a novel.

Your temperament also dictates which areas of investment are most suitable for you. If you are a risk taker, you will be bored and restless holding such long-term investments such as unit trusts or certificates of deposit. You may be tempted to make quick decisions before all the risks have been considered, leading to second-guessing and excessive portfolio turnover.

In formulating your business plan for living, the element of time is the single thing beyond your control; however, the time available for each aspect of your life is within your control. When we are young, time seems endless, and it is easy to postpone important decisions. No one can say how long you will live, but it can be said with certainty that you can never retrieve yesterday. Plan your available time now so that tomorrow will bring no regrets for squandered yesterdays.

Investments made as a result of thoughtful planning have proved to offer the best chance for success. As the CEO of your life, it is up to you to make an inventory of your assets, to set long-term goals, and to formulate a business plan for reaching those goals.

2. Know Your Investments

Before placing your money at risk, you should thoroughly study all aspects of an investment. Know the mechanics involved and be aware of any potential problems. When dealing with foreign securities, know the potential political changes that can affect business. Watch the currency markets for early signs of economic changes that are not revealed in statistics. Remember, statistics only reveal the past, while successful investing must foretell the future with reasonable accuracy.

Risk is part of life, and there is no investment that is totally risk free. To hold long-term bonds or CDs in inflationary environments produces risk almost to a certainty, while holding real estate in a deflationary environment will produce equally disastrous results. Learn the special risks associated with each potential investment before you act. Know the liquidity, how easy it is to get out, before committing funds. Know how to neutralize special risks through hedging; for example, shorting currencies against real estate. Because you can never be free of risk, expect to make mistakes. Mistakes are part of investing. Learn from your mistakes and make the promise to never make the same mistake a second time.

3. Nobody Will Watch Your Money the Way You Will

Money managers are helpful for those who do not have the time to devote to properly studying each potential investment. However, it is important that both the manager (this includes the mutual fund manager) and the investor have a clear agreement as to the goals and the methods they will employ. Without such an understanding, disappointment is almost certain.

You must be realistic in your expectations. To ask a money manager to provide a portfolio that pays high dividends, that has a growth of capital better than the Standard & Poor's 500, and that still offers 100 percent protection against down markets is unrealistic. Yet, these are the expectations of many who purchase mutual funds. It is up to you to find the manager that has a style compatible with your goals and objectives. If no manager can be found to match your expectations, perhaps your expectations need to be examined.

Unless you have millions to put under management, you cannot expect the money manager to tailor the portfolio to your individual desires. You will be part of a group of investors that is generally homogeneous, but each investor has goals and objectives that differ from the rest of the group. When you give up control of your money to gain time, you also relinquish the right to complain about specific judgments made by the money manager. You do have the right to complain when the manager varies from the broad guidelines for investments that were outlined to you when you deposited your money.

The foregoing points are particularly important when foreign markets are included in your portfolio. Although most money managers have vast amounts of information that may be overlooked by the U.S. press, their calculations about overseas investments may be quickly negated by unanticipated events such as revolutions, coups, and major bank failures. Under those circumstances, the investor is best guided by restraint and patience. A good money manager can salvage a great deal and, if given sufficient time, perhaps even profit from what first appears to be a disastrous event.

4. The Warm, Cozy Feeling of Home

The fear of the unexpected keeps most investors from considering the opportunities in foreign markets. Familiarity breeds complacency, and the average investor feels comfortable keeping his money near home, even when his intellect determines that far better investments are available abroad. Advisers have relied on the theme of diversification to induce their clients to commit some portion of investment funds to foreign markets. Diversification promises increased safety and increased yield, but the true gain in a portfolio is increased opportunity.

5. Guarantees Come at a Price

FDIC insurance was intended to protect small savers from losing everything in the event of a bank failure. It was not intended to shelter investors from the results of poor investment strategies. Generally, insurance premiums are paid by the owner of a policy, but in the case of FDIC coverage, the costs are borne by the member banks. The insurance that covers your deposit in a foreign-denominated currency account at a U.S. bank is a marvelous gift to you. Use it to your advantage.

6. Adventures Abroad

Taking your first step into the waters of international investing is an exhilarating adventure. You find all of your senses sharpened as you cautiously make your way along an uncharted shore, alert for any warning of deep holes that might plunge you in water over your head. You become annoyed by the scant coverage given to foreign news in your local paper, and outright belligerent toward the TV reporters that waste time on a small fire when an important election is being decided in Germany or Japan. Gradually, you begin to seek information in *The Wall Street Journal, The New York Times, Foreign Affairs,* and the *Economist.* Your world has expanded and the various pronouncements of Washington politicians take on new meaning.

7. Don't Call It "Funny Money"

The tendency of the individual traveler abroad is to relegate foreign currencies to the status of play money. The concept that 3,000 Italian lira or 1,000 Japanese yen could actually be useful in buying a meal seems foreign to the American who grew up with dollars. Yet, this is the stuff for which people work, the stuff they use to pay their taxes, and the stuff they exchange for dollars when they buy American goods. Knowledge of the relative values of the world's currencies in relation to the dollar is a first step in becoming a successful global investor.

8. Leverage—A Two-Edged Sword

Intelligent speculation concentrates investments in areas most likely to provide a significant increase to the capital base. The use of leverage (borrowing) increases the rate of increase of a successful investment, but can produce substantial losses when improperly employed. The twin devils of fear and greed are at home in all markets. Greed can often lead to the reckless use of leverage, and fear of loss from an overleveraged position can lead to heedless abandonment of that position. Intelligent speculation on margin is the key to large gains, but unintelligent speculation will certainly lead to large losses if leverage is employed. Know your investment well before employing leverage.

9. Economics: The Dismal Science

The first principal of economics should be: Everything is open to question. Complex problems are often simplified to the point where most truth has been wrung out, leaving only that aspect that best illustrates the particular view of the economist speaking. TV commentators love those comments that provide explanations of world events in a sound bite. Unfortunately, such simplifications are often accepted as valid appraisals by the public, leading to conclusions that are detrimental to the best interests of the United States and the world.

Consider the fable at the end of Chapter 2. It illustrated the concept of comparative advantage but, in its simplification, eliminates many complexities of the problem. Some of the questions left unanswered are:

- Who would decide what product should be produced to the exclusion of some other product? Does this not imply centralized planning?
- How would the economic gains, made through concentrating on those goods with a comparative advantage, be used? Would the prince build a new castle? Would the princess establish a national retirement plan? Would the workers receive more pay?
- How do you provide for the workers who see their jobs shifted to a foreign country? Cobblers cannot become farmers overnight, nor can farmers become cobblers through a national

decree. Would all of the gains made be spent on retraining? When international trade expands, the total number of jobs increases, but displacement of workers occurs as each nation seeks to expand industries in which it has a comparative advantage.

Learn to ask questions whenever a simplified explanation is offered to a complex problem. Why is one currency weak and another strong? If you are told that it is the result of speculation, look further. Why does the French market rally despite the release of increased unemployment data? If you are told that the socialists are gaining ground, look further. Remember, when markets move contrary to reason, check your reasons.

10. Investing with Currency Trends

Despite all of the foregoing, you will find that the one indispensable tool for guiding your investments lies in your local paper. There, buried at the back of the financial pages, you will find the listing of daily changes in the value of the dollar as it relates to other major world currencies. As you follow these tables daily, you will gain a sense of which economy is progressing and which is falling behind. With this knowledge, you will find an increasing ability to discover hitherto unsuspected opportunities for successful investment. Never fight the trend of a currency. Remember, the trend is your friend. Never doubt it.

For the U.S. investor, to maximize profits, purchases of foreign investments should be made during periods of dollar strength (more shares per dollar), and sales made during periods of dollar weakness (more dollars per share). Whether you place your funds in foreign-currency denominated certificates of deposit, dollar denominated American depository receipts, international mutual funds, or a futures account, your chances for success are greatly multiplied. You have discovered the currency key.

◆ APPENDIX A ◆

Open-End Global Bond Funds

Open-End Global Bond Funds

Name of Fund	Telephone	Minimum Investment	Maximum Sales Charge (% of offering price)
Alliance Multimarket Strategy Trust*	800-247-4154	$ 250	4.25
Alliance Short-Term Multi Market*	800-247-4154	$ 250	4.25
Alliance World Income Trust*	800-247-4154	$ 10,000	no-load
American Capital Global Government	800-421-5666	$ 500	4.75
API Trust-Global Income	800-544-6060	$ 500	no-load
BB&K International Fixed Income	800-882-8383	$ 5,000	no-load
BJB Global Income	800-435-4659	$ 2,500	4.00
Blanchard Short-Term Global	800-922-7771	$ 3,000	no-load
Bull & Bear Global Income	800-847-4200	$ 1,000	no-load
Capital World Bond Fund	800-421-4120	$ 1,000	4.75
Compass Capital International Fixed Income	800-451-8371	$ 2,500	3.75

Name of Fund	Telephone	Minimum Investment	Maximum Sales Charge (% of offering price)
Comstock Partners Strategy "O"	800-654-6561	$ 2,500	4.50
Dean Witter Global Short-Term	800-869-3863	$ 1,000	3.00
Dean Witter World Wide Income	800-869-3863	$ 1,000	5.00
DFA Global Fixed Income	800-395-8005	$ 100,000	no-load
Eaton Vance Short-Term Global	800-225-6265	$ 1,000	3.00
FFTW Worldwide Fixed Income	800-762-4848	$ 100,000	no-load
FFTW Worldwide Fixed Income Hedge	800-762-4848	$ 100,000	no-load
Fidelity Global Bond	800-544-8888	$ 2,500	no-load
Fidelity Short-Term World	800-544-8888	$ 2,500	no-load
FLWX Fund Short-Term Global*	800-325-3539	$ 2,500	no-load
Franklin Inv. Global Government Income	800-342-5236	$ 100	4.25
Franklin Partners Tax-Advantage	800-342-5236	$ 2,500	4.25
Franklin/Templeton Global Currency*	800-632-2301	$ 100	3.00
Franklin/Templeton Hard Currency*	800-632-2301	$ 100	3.00
Franklin/Templeton High Income	800-632-2301	$ 100	3.00
G.T. Global Government Income	800-548-9994	$ 500	4.75
G.T. Global Strategic A	800-548-9994	$ 500	4.75
G.T. High Income	800-548-9994	$ 500	4.75
Glenmede International Fixed Income	800-442-8299	$ 25,000	no-load
Govett Government Income	800-634-6838	$ 500	4.95
IDS Global Bond A	800-328-8300	$ 2,000	5.00
J. Hancock Global Income	800-225-6020	$ 1,000	4.00
J. Hancock Short-Term Strategic	800-225-6020	$ 1,000	3.00
J. Hancock Strategic Income A	800-225-6020	$ 1,000	4.50
Kemper Global Income A	800-621-1048	$ 1,000	4.50

Name of Fund	Telephone	Minimum Investment	Maximum Sales Charge (% of offering price)
Keystone America World Bond	800-343-2898	$ 1,000	4.75
Kidder Peabody Global Fixed A	212-510-3000	$ 5,000	2.25
Loomis Sayles Global Bond	800-633-3330	$ 2,500	no-load
Lord Abbett Global Income	800-426-1130	$ 1,000	4.75
Merrill Lynch Global Bond A	800-637-3863	$ 1,000	4.00
Merrill Lynch Global Convertible	800-637-3863	$ 1,000	5.25
Merrill Lynch Short-Term Global	800-637-3863	$ 1,000	3.00
Merrill Lynch World Income A	800-637-3863	$ 1,000	4.00
MFS Intermediate Income A	800-343-2829	$ 1,000	4.75
MFS World Governments A	800-343-2829	$ 1,000	4.75
Paine Webber Global Income	800-647-1568	$ 1,000	4.00
Pegasus International Bond	800-688-3350	$ 1,000	4.50
Pilgram Short-Term Multi Market	800-334-3444	$ 5,000	3.00
PIMCO Foreign Fund	800-927-4648	$1,000,000	no-load
Price (T. Rowe) Global Government	800-638-5660	$ 2,500	no-load
Price (T. Rowe) International Bond	800-638-5660	$ 2,500	no-load
Price (T. Rowe) Short-Term Global	800-638-5660	$ 2,500	no-load
Prudential Intermediate Global A	800-225-1852	$ 1,000	3.00
Prudential Short-Term Global Assets	800-225-1852	$ 1,000	0.99
Prudential Short-Term Global Income	800-225-1852	$ 1,000	3.00
Putnam Global Government Income A	800-232-3863	$ 500	4.75

Name of Fund	Telephone	Minimum Investment	Maximum Sales Charge (% of offering price)
Quest for Value Global Income A	800-232-3863	$ 1,000	3.00
Scudder International Bond	800-225-2470	$ 1,000	no-load
Scudder Short-Term Global	800-225-2470	$ 1,000	no-load
Seven Seas Yield Plus*	800-647-7327	$ 1,000	no-load
Sierra Trust Short-Term Global Government	800-222-5852	$ 250	3.50
Smith Barney Global Government Bond A	800-221-8806	$ 10,000	4.50
Templeton Income Fund	800-237-0738	$ 100	4.25
Van Eck Global Income A	800-221-2220	$ 1,000	4.75
Van Kampen Short-Term Global A	800-225-2222	$ 1,000	3.00
Waddell & Reed Global Income	913-236-2000	$ 1,000	3.00
Warburg Pincus Global Fixed	800-257-5614	$ 2,500	no-load

*A secondary objective is the use of currency fluctuations to improve investment results.

◆ APPENDIX B ◆

Open-End Global and International Equity Funds

Open-End Global and International Equity Funds

Name of Fund	Telephone	Minimum Investment	Maximum Sales Charge (% of offering price)
Acorn International Fund	800-922-6769	$ 1,000	no-load
Aetna International Growth	800-367-7732	$ 1,000	no-load
AIM International Equity A	800-347-1919	$ 500	5.50
Alliance Global Small Cap A	800-247-4154	$ 250	4.25
Alliance International A	800-247-4154	$ 250	4.25
Ambassador International Stock Ret A	800-892-4366	$ 500	3.75
American A Advantage International Equity	800-967-3509	$ 10,000	no-load
American Capital Global Equity	800-421-5666	$ 500	5.75
Babson-Stewart Ivory International	800-422-2766	$ 2,500	no-load
Bartlett Value International Fund	800-800-4612	$ 5,000	no-load

Name of Fund	Telephone	Minimum Investment	Maximum Sales Charge (% of offering price)
BB&K International Equity	800-882-8383	$ 5,000	no-load
Blanchard Global Growth	800-922-7771	$ 3,000	no-load
Brinson Fund-Global	800-448-2430	$ 100,000	no-load
Bull & Bear U.S. and Overseas	800-847-4200	$ 1,000	no-load
Calvert World Value Global Equity	800-368-2745	$ 2,000	4.75
Colonial Global Equity	800-345-6611	$ 1,000	5.75
Colonial International Fund for Growth	800-345-6611	$ 1,000	5.75
Columbia International Stock	800-547-1707	$ 1,000	no-load
CoreFund International Growth	800-355-2673	$1,000,000	no-load
Dean Witter World Wide Trust	800-869-3863	$ 1,000	5.00
Delaware Group International Equity	800-523-4640	$ 250	5.75
DFA Large Cap International	310-395-8005	$2,000,000	no-load
Dreyfus Global Growth Fund	800-782-6620	$ 2,500	3.00
Dreyfus Premier Global Investors	800-645-6561	$ 2,500	4.50
Elfun Global Fund	800-242-0134	$ 100	no-load
Enterprise International Growth	800-432-4320	$ 1,000	4.75
Evergreen Global Real Estate	800-235-0064	$ 2,000	no-load
Fidelity Advisors Global Resources	800-522-7297	$ 1,000	4.75
Fidelity Advisors Overseas Fund	800-522-7297	$ 1,000	4.75
Fidelity Diversified International Fund	800-544-8888	$ 2,500	no-load
Fidelity Emerging Markets	800-544-8888	$ 2,500	3.00
Fidelity International Growth & Income	800-544-8888	$ 2,500	no-load
Fidelity Overseas Fund	800-544-8888	$ 2,500	3.00
First Investors Global Fund	800-423-4026	$ 2,000	6.25

Name of Fund	Telephone	Minimum Investment	Maximum Sales Charge (% of offering price)
Flag Investors International Fund	800-767-3524	$ 2,000	4.50
Fortis Worldwide Global Growth	800-800-2638	$ 500	4.75
Founders Passport Fund	888-217-8100	$ 1,000	no-load
Founders Worldwide Growth	888-217-8100	$ 1,000	no-load
Franklin International Equity	800-632-2301	$ 100	4.50
Fremont Global Fund	800-548-4539	$ 2,000	no-load
G.T. Emerging Markets	800-548-9994	$ 500	4.75
G.T. Global Growth & Income	800-548-9994	$ 500	4.75
G.T. International Growth	800-548-9994	$ 500	4.75
G.T. Worldwide Growth	800-548-9994	$ 500	4.75
Galaxy International Equity	800-628-0414	$ 2,500	no-load
GAM Global Fund	800-426-4685	$ 10,000	5.00
GAM International Fund	800-426-4685	$ 10,000	5.00
Glenmede International Fund	800-442-8299	$ 25,000	no-load
Govett International Equity	800-634-6838	$ 500	4.95
Loomis Sayles International Equity	800-633-3330	$ 2,500	no-load
Lord Abbett Global Equity	800-426-1130	$ 1,000	5.75
MainStay Global Fund	800-522-4202	$ 500	5.00
Managers International Equity	800-835-3879	$ 10,000	no-load
Merrill Lynch Developing Capital	800-637-3863	$ 5,000	5.25
Merrill Lynch Global Allocation	800-637-3863	$ 1,000	5.25
Merrill Lynch Global Holdings	800-637-3863	$ 1,000	5.25
MetLife Portfolio-International Equity	800-882-0052	$ 500	no-load
MFS World Equity	800-343-2829	$ 1,000	5.75
MFS World Growth	800-343-2829	$ 1,000	5.75
MFS World Total Return	800-343-2829	$ 1,000	5.75
Montgomery Global Opportunities	800-428-1871	$ 1,000	no-load

Name of Fund	Telephone	Minimum Investment	Maximum Sales Charge (% of offering price)
Morgan Stanley Global Equities	800-548-7786	$ 1,000	4.75
Nations International Equity Investors	800-982-2271	$ 1,000	5.75
Nations International Equity Trust	800-982-2271	$ 1,000	no-load
New Perspective Fund	800-421-4120	$ 250	5.75
North American Global Growth	617-266-6004	$ 1,000	no-load
Oakmark International Fund	800-625-6275	$ 2,500	no-load
Oppenheimer Global Emerging Growth	800-525-7040	$ 25	5.75
Oppenheimer Global Fund	800-525-7040	$ 25	5.75
Oppenheimer Global Growth & Income	800-525-7040	$ 25	5.75
PaineWebber Atlas Global Growth	800-647-1568	$ 1,000	4.50
PaineWebber Global Growth & Income	800-647-1568	$ 1,000	4.00
Parkstone International Discovery Fund	800-451-8377	$ 1,000	4.50
Phoenix International Portfolio	800-243-1574	$ 500	4.75
Phoenix Worldwide Opportunities	800-243-1574	$ 500	4.75
Piper Jaffray Global-Pacific-Europe	800-333-6000	$ 250	4.00
PNC Fund-International Equity	800-422-6538	$ 5,000	no-load
PNC Fund-International Investors	800-422-6538	$ 500	4.50
Preferred International Fund	800-662-4768	$ 1,000	no-load
Price (T. Rowe) International Stock	800-638-5660	$ 2,500	no-load
Price (T. Rowe) International Discovery	800-638-5660	$ 2,500	no-load
Princor World Fund	800-247-4123	$ 300	4.75
Prudential Global Fund	800-225-1852	$ 1,000	5.00
Prudential Global Genesis	800-225-1852	$ 1,000	5.00

Name of Fund	Telephone	Minimum Investment	Maximum Sales Charge (% of offering price)
Prudential Global Utility	800-225-1852	$ 1,000	5.00
Putnam Global Growth Fund	800-225-1581	$ 500	5.75
Quantitative Group-International Equity	800-331-1244	$ 5,000	1.00
Quest for Value Global Equity	800-232-3863	$ 1,000	5.50
Regis TS&W International Equity	800-638-7983	$ 100,000	no-load
Retirement Plan America Global Value	800-279-2279	$ 1,000	4.75
Rodney Square International	800-336-9970	$ 1,000	4.00
Schroder International Equity	800-344-8332	$ 2,500	no-load
Scottish Widows International Fund	800-523-5903	$ 1,000	4.75
Scudder Global Fund	800-225-2470	$ 1,000	no-load
Scudder International Fund	800-225-2470	$ 1,000	no-load
Seligman Henderson Global Small Cap	800-221-7844	$ 1,000	4.75
Seligman Henderson International	800-221-7844	$ 1,000	4.75
Sentinel World Fund	800-282-3863	$ 500	5.00
Sierra Trust International Growth	800-222-5852	$ 250	4.50
SIT International Growth Fund	800-332-5580	$ 2,000	no-load
SMALLCAP World Fund	800-421-4129	$ 1,000	5.75
Smith Barney International Equity	800-221-8806	$ 3,000	5.00
SoGen Interhantional Fund	800-334-2143	no minimum	3.75
Standish Fund International Equity	617-350-6100	$ 50,000	no-load
Strong International Stock	800-368-1030	$ 1,000	no-load
Templeton Developing Markets	800-237-0738	$ 100	5.75
Templeton Foreign Fund	800-237-0738	$ 100	5.75
Templeton Global Opportunity	800-237-0738	$ 100	5.75

Name of Fund	Telephone	Minimum Investment	Maximum Sales Charge (% of offering price)
Templeton Growth Fund	800-237-0738	$ 100	5.75
Templeton Smaller Company's Growth	800-237-0738	$ 100	5.75
Templeton World Fund	800-237-0738	$ 100	5.75
Tocqueville Euro-Pacific Fund	800-697-3863	$ 5,000	no-load
Twentieth Century International Equity	800-345-2021	$ 2,500	no-load
United International Growth	800-366-5465	$ 500	5.75
UST Master International	800-233-1136	$ 1,000	4.50
Van Eck World Trends	800-221-2220	$ 1,000	4.75
Vanguard International Growth Portfolio	800-662-7447	$ 3,000	no-load
Vanguard Trustees' Equity-International	800-662-7447	$ 10,000	no-load
Vontobel EuroPacific Fund	800-527-9500	$ 1,000	no-load
Warburg Pincus International Equity	800-257-5614	$ 2,500	no-load
WPG International	800-223-3332	$ 2,500	no-load
Wright International Blue-Chip Equity	800-232-0013	$ 1,000	no-load
Yamaichi Global Fund	800-257-0228	$ 1,000	4.75

◆ APPENDIX C ◆

Regional Mutual Funds

Income (Bond) Funds

Name of Fund	Telephone	Minimum Investment	Maximum Sales Charge (% of investment)
Benham European Government Bond	800-321-8321	$ 1,000	no-load
TCW/DW North American Government	800-869-3863	$ 1,000	no-load

Equity (Stock) Funds

Name of Fund	Telephone	Minimum Investment	Maximum Sales Charge (% of investment)
59 Wall St. European Equity	212-493-8100	$25,000	no-load
59 Wall St. Pacific Basin Equity	212-493-8100	$25,000	no-load
Alliance New Europe	800-247-4154	$ 250	4.25
Dean Witter European Growth	800-869-3863	$ 1,000	5.00

Name of Fund	Telephone	Minimum Investment	Maximum Sales Charge (% of investment)
Dean Witter Pacific Growth	800-869-3863	$ 1,000	5.00
DFA Continental Small Company	310-345-8005	$ 2,000	no-load
EuroPacific Growth Fund	800-421-4120	$ 250	5.75
Fidelity Europe	800-544-8888	$ 2,500	3.00
Fidelity Pacific Basin	800-544-8888	$ 2,500	3.00
Franklin Pacific Growth	800-632-2301	$ 100	4.50
G.T. Europe Growth Fund	800-548-9994	$ 500	4.75
G.T. Latin America Growth	800-548-9994	$ 500	4.75
G.T. Pacific Growth Fund	800-548-9994	$ 500	4.75
GAM Europe Fund	800-426-4685	$10,000	5.00
GAM North America Fund	800-426-4685	$10,000	5.00
GAM Pacific Basin Fund	800-426-4685	$10,000	5.00
INVESCO European Fund	800-525-8085	$ 1,000	no-load
INVESCO Pacific Basin Fund	800-525-8085	$ 1,000	no-load
J. Hancock Pacific Basin	800-225-6020	$ 1,000	5.00
Merrill Lynch Dragon Fund	800-637-3863	$ 1,000	4.00
Merrill Lych Eurofund	800-637-3863	$ 500	5.25
Merrill Lynch Latin America	800-637-3863	$ 1,000	4.00
Merrill Lynch Pacific Fund	800-637-3863	$ 250	5.25
Morgan Stanley Asian Growth	800-548-7786	$ 1,000	4.75
Newport Tiger Fund	800-527-9500	$ 1,000	5.00
Nomura Pacific Basin Fund	800-833-0018	$ 1,000	no-load
Paine Webber Europe Growth	800-647-1568	$ 1,000	4.50
Pioneer Europe Growth	800-638-5660	$ 1,000	5.75
Price (T. Rowe) European Stock	800-638-5660	$ 2,500	no-load
Price (T. Rowe) New Asia Fund	800-638-5660	$ 2,500	no-load
Prudential Pacific Growth	800-225-1852	$ 1,000	5.00
Putnam Asia Pacific	800-225-1581	$ 500	5.75
Putnam Europe Growth	800-225-1581	$ 500	5.75

Name of Fund	Telephone	Minimum Investment	Maximum Sales Charge (% of investment)
Scudder Latin American Fund	800-225-2470	$ 1,000	no-load
Scudder Pacific Opportunities	800-225-2470	$ 1,000	no-load
TCW/DW Latin American Growth	800-869-3863	$ 1,000	5.00
Vanguard International Equity Index (Europe)	800-662-7447	$ 3,000	no-load
Vanguard International Equity Index (Pacific)	800-662-7447	$ 3,000	no-load

◆ A P P E N D I X   D ◆

Single-Country Mutual Funds

Income (Bond) Funds

Name of Fund	Telephone	Minimum Investment	Maximum Sales Charge (% of investment)
Franklin/Templeton German Government	800-632-2301	$ 100	3.00
Keystone Australia Income Fund	800-343-2898	$1,000	4.75

Equity (Stock) Funds

Name of Fund	Telephone	Minimum Investment	Maximum Sales Charge (% of investment)
Capstone New Zealand Fund	800-262-6631	$ 200	4.75
Capstone Nikko Japan Fund	800-262-6631	$ 200	4.75
DFA Japanese Small Companies	800-395-8005	$2,000	no-load

Name of Fund	Telephone	Minimum Investment	Maximum Sales Charge (% of investment)
Eaton Vance Traditional China	800-225-6265	$1,000	4.75
Fidelity Canada Fund	800-544-8888	$2,500	no-load
Fidelity Japan Fund	800-544-8888	$2,500	no-load
G.T. Japan Growth Fund	800-548-9994	$ 500	4.75
Japan Fund	800-225-2470	$1,000	no-load
Lexington Troika Russia	800-526-0056	$1,000	no-load
Price (T. Rowe) Japan Fund	800-638-5660	$2,500	no-load

◆ A P P E N D I X E ◆

Closed-End Funds

Closed-End Global and International Bond Funds

Name of Fund	Symbol	Market	Manager
ACM Managed Multi-Market	MMF	NYSE	Alliance Capital
Dreyfus Strategic Government	DSI	NYSE	Dreyfus
Emerging Markets Floating Rate	EFL	NYSE	Salomon Bros.
Emerging Markets Income	EFL	NYSE	Advantage Advisors
Global Government Plus	GOV	NYSE	Prudential
Global High Income Dollar Fund	GHI	NYSE	Mitchell Hutchins
Global Partners Income	GDF	NYSE	Salomon Bros.
Global Total Return	PGY	NYSE	Prudential
Morgan Stanley Emerging Debt	MSD	NYSE	Morgan Stanley
Morgan Stanley Global Opportunity Bond	MGB	NYSE	Morgan Stanley
Salomon 2008 World Wide Government	SBG	NYSE	Salomon Bros.
Salomon World Wide Income	SBW	NYSE	Salomon Bros.
Scudder World Income Opportunity	SWI	NYSE	Scudder Stevens
Strategic Global Income	SGL	NYSE	Mitchell Hutchins
Templeton Emerging Markets Income	TEI	NYSE	Templeton
Templeton Global Government	TGG	NYSE	Templeton

Name of Fund	Symbol	Market	Manager
Templeton Global Income	GIM	NYSE	Templeton
Worldwide $ Vest	WDV	NYSE	Fund Asset Management

Closed-End Global and International Equity Funds

Name of Fund	Symbol	Market	Manager
Clemente Global Growth	CLM	NYSE	Clemente Capital
Emerging Markets Infrastructure	EMG	NYSE	BEA Associates
G.T. Developing Markets	G.T.D	NYSE	G.T. Capital
Global Small Cap	GSG	NYSE	Mitchell Hutchins
Morgan Stanley Emerging Markets	MSF	NYSE	Morgan Stanley
TCW/DW Emerging Markets	EMO	NYSE	TCW Management
Worldwide Value	VLU	NYSE	Lombard Order

Closed-End Regional Funds

Regional funds are more restrictive on the managers, generally requiring that a large percentage of the portfolio be invested within a specific area. When considering an investment in a regional fund, remember that the area often mirrors the economic progress of the country that controls the currency used for settling trades.

Closed-End Regional Bond Funds

Name of Fund	Symbol	Market	Manager
America's Income Trust	XUS	NYSE	Piper Capital
Black Rock North American Government	BNA	NYSE	BlackRock Financial
Latin American Dollar Income	LBF	NYSE	Scudder Stevens

Closed-End Regional Equity Funds

Name of Fund	Symbol	Market	Manager
America's All Seasons Fund	FUND	Nasdaq	Veitia & Associates
Asia Pacific Fund	APB	NYSE	Baring International
Asia Tigers Fund	GRR	NYSE	Barclays de Zoete
Emerging Tigers Fund	TGF	NYSE	Merrill Lynch
Europe Fund	EF	NYSE	Warburg Investment
European Warrant Fund	EWF	NYSE	Julius Baer
Fidelity Emerging Asia Fund	FAE	NYSE	Fidelity
Foreign & Colonial Emerging Middle East	EME	NYSE	Foreign & Colonial
G.T. Greater Europe Fund	GTF	NYSE	G.T. Capital
Herzfeld Caribbean Basin Fund	CUBA	Nasdaq	Herzfeld/Cuba
Latin America Discovery Fund	LDF	NYSE	Morgan Stanley
Latin American Equity Fund	LAQ	NYSE	BEA Associates
Latin American Investment Fund	LAM	NYSE	BEA Associates
Lehman Bros. Latin American Growth	LLF	NYSE	Lehman Bros.
Morgan Stanley Africa Fund	AFF	NYSE	Morgan Stanley
Morgan Stanley Asia Pacific	APF	NYSE	Morgan Stanley
Morgan Stanley Russia & New Europe	RNE	NYSE	Morgan Stanley
Scudder New Asia Fund	SAF	NYSE	Scudder Stevens
Scudder New Europe Fund	NEF	NYSE	Scudder Stevens
Southern Africa Fund	SOA	NYSE	Alliance Capital
TCW/DW Emerging Markets	EMO	NYSE	TCW Funds Management
Templeton Dragon Fund	TDF	NYSE	Templeton Investment
Templeton Emerging Markets Appreciation	TEA	NYSE	Templeton Investment

Closed-End Single-Country Equity Funds

Name of Fund	Symbol	Market	Manager
Argentina Fund	AF	NYSE	Scudder Stevens
ASA Limited	ASA	NYSE	ASA Ltd. Management
Austria Fund	OST	NYSE	Alliance Capital
Brazil Fund	BZF	NYSE	Scudder Stevens
Brazilian Equity Fund	BZL	NYSE	BEA Associates
Chile Fund	CH	NYSE	BEA Associates
China Fund	CHN	NYSE	Wardley Investment
Czech Republic	CRF	NYSE	Advantage Investors
Emerging Germany	FRG	NYSE	Dresdner Bank
Emerging Mexico	MEF	NYSE	Santander Managment
Fidelity Advisors Korea	FAK	NYSE	Fidelity
First Australia Fund	IAF	NYSE	EquiLink
First Iberian Fund	IBF	NYSE	Scudder Stevens
First Israel Fund	ISL	NYSE	BEA Associates
First Philippine Fund	FPF	NYSE	Clemente Capital
France Growth Fund	FRF	NYSE	Indosuez International
Future German Fund	FGF	NYSE	Deutsche Asset Management
Germany Fund	GER	NYSE	Deutsche Asset Management
Germany Emerging Growth	FRG	NYSE	Dresdner Bank
Greater China Fund	GCH	NYSE	Baring International
Growth Fund Spain	GSP	NYSE	Kemper Financial
India Fund	IFN	NYSE	Barclays de Zoete
India Growth Fund	IGF	NYSE	Unit Trust of India
Indonesia Fund	IF	NYSE	BEA Associates
Irish Investment Fund	IRL	NYSE	Bank of Ireland
Italy Fund	ITA	NYSE	Lehman Bros.
Jakarta Growth Fund	JHF	NYSE	Nomura Capital
Japan Equity Fund	JEQ	NYSE	Daiwa Investments
Japan OTC Equity Fund	JOF	NYSE	Nomura Capital
Jardine Fleming China	JFC	NYSE	Jardine Fleming
Jardine Fleming India	JFI	NYSE	Jardine Fleming
Korea Fund	KF	NYSE	Scudder Stevens
Korea Equity Fund	KEF	NYSE	Nomura Capital
Korea Investment Fund	KIF	NYSE	Alliance Capital
Malaysia Fund	MF	NYSE	Morgan Stanley
Mexico Fund	MXF	NYSE	Impulsora del Fondo
Mexico Equity & Income	MXE	NYSE	Advantage Advisors
Morgan Stanley India Fund	IIF	NYSE	Morgan Stanley

Name of Fund	Symbol	Market	Manager
New Germany Fund	GF	NYSE	Deutche Asset Management
New South Africa Fund	NSA	NYSE	Robert Fleming, Inc.
Pakistan Investment	PKF	NYSE	Morgan Stanley
Portugal Fund	PGF	NYSE	BEA Associates
ROC Taiwan Fund	ROC	NYSE	International Investment Trust
Singapore Fund	SGF	NYSE	DBS Management
Spain Fund	SNF	NYSE	Alliance Capital
Swiss Helvetia Fund	SWZ	NYSE	Hottinger Capital
Taiwan Equity	TYN	NYSE	Daiwa Investments
Taiwan Fund	TWN	NYSE	China Securities
Templeton China	TCH	NYSE	Templeton Investment
Templeton Russia	TRF	NYSE	Templeton Investment
Templeton Vietnam	TVF	NYSE	Templeton Investment
Thai Capital Fund	TC	NYSE	Mutual Fund Co., Ltd.
Thai Fund	TTF	NYSE	Morgan Stanley
Turkish Investment Fund	TKF	NYSE	Morgan Stanley

APPENDIX F

U.S.-Based
Multinational Companies

The following list contains U.S. companies with 50 percent or more of their revenues derived from overseas operations. Had the parameters been set at companies with more than 40 percent of sales from abroad, it would have been twice as long. Even so, it is by no means complete. You can see how dependent on international trading the U.S. economy has become.

Company	Symbol	Exchange	Business	% of Revenues (from overseas)
AMP, Inc.	AMP	NYSE	Electrical Connectors	60
Able Telcom Holding	ABTE	Nasdaq	Telephone	51
Advance Ross	AROS	Nasdaq	Duty Free Shops	97
AFLAC	AFL	NYSE	Health Insurance	84
Air Express International	AEIC	Nasdaq	Air Freight	57
American Brands	AMB	NYSE	Tobacco, Foods	64
American International Group	AIG	NYSE	Insurance	52
American Standard	ASD	NYSE	Air-Conditioning	50
Andros, Inc.	ANDY	Nasdaq	Instrumentation	63
Aptargroup	ATR	NYSE	Containers	60

Company	Symbol	Exchange	Business	% of Revenues (from overseas)
Atwood Oceanics	ATW	Nasdaq	Offshore Oil Drilling	92
Autodesk, Inc.	ACAD	Nasdaq	Software (CAD)	61
Avon Products	AVP	NYSE	Cosmetics	64
BTU International	BTUI	Nasdaq	Thermal Processing	52
Berlitz International	BTZ	NYSE	Language Instruction	73
Biopool International	BIPL	Nasdaq	Blood Testing Kits	60
Boeing Co.	BA	NYSE	Aircraft Manufacture	54
CBI Industries	CBI	NYSE	Carbon Dioxide Gas	53
CPC International	CPC	NYSE	Food Processing	61
Cadence Design	CDN	NYSE	Automation Software	52
Cambrex Corp.	CBEX	Nasdaq	Computer Memory	75
Caterpillar, Inc.	CAT	NYSE	Earthmoving Machinery	50
Chevron Corp.	CHV	NYSE	Integrated Petroleum	60
Chrysler Corp.	C	NYSE	Motor Vehicles	50
Coca-Cola	KO	NYSE	Soft Drinks	68
Colgate-Palmolive	CL	NYSE	Consumer Products	69
COMPAQ Computer	CPQ	NYSE	Desktop Computers	50
Daniel Industries	DAN	NYSE	Fluid Control Devices	60
Digital Equipment	DEC	NYSE	Computers	62
Dow Chemical	DOW	NYSE	Chemicals	50
Eastman Kodak	EK	NYSE	Photographic Supplies	53
Exxon Corp.	XON	NYSE	Integrated Petroleum	65
Ferro Corp.	FOE	NYSE	Specialty Materials	50
Gillette Co.	G	NYSE	Toiletries	68
Great Lakes Chemical	GLK	NYSE	Specialty Chemicals	55
Hewlett Packard	HWP	NYSE	Computer Products	54

Company	Symbol	Exchange	Business	% of Revenues (from overseas)
IBM	IBM	NYSE	Computer Products	59
International Specialty Products	ISP	NYSE	Chemicals	50
Interpool, Inc.	IPX	NYSE	Container Leasing	90
Keystone International	KII	NYSE	Valves	57
KLA-Tencor	KLAC	Nasdaq	Electronics Quality Control	65
K-Tron International	KTII	Nasdaq	Gravimetric Feeders	70
Lawter International	LAW	NYSE	Printing Equipment	50
Loctite Corporation	LOC	NYSE	Engineering Adhesives	58
Lubrizol Corporation	LZ	NYSE	Lubricants	56
Mattel, Inc.	MAT	NYSE	Toys/Dolls	50
McDermott (J. Ray)	JRM	NYSE	Marine Construction	71
McDonald's Corporation	MCD	NYSE	Fast Food Franchising	50
Measurex Corporation	MX	NYSE	Paper-Manufacturing Systems	57
Millipore Corporation	MIL	NYSE	Specialized Filters	64
Minnesota Mining	MMM	NYSE	Consumer Products	50
Mobil Corporation	MOB	NYSE	Integrated Petroleum	77
NL Industries	NL	NYSE	Pigments (titanium)	73
National Semiconductor	NSM	NYSE	Semiconductors	56
Oceaneering International	OII	NYSE	Offshore Oil Drilling	61
Omnicom Group	OMC	NYSE	Advertising	51
Pall Corporation	PLL	NYSE	Disposable Filters	57
Perkin Elmer	PKN	NYSE	Life Science Systems	59
Polaroid Corporation	PRD	NYSE	Instant Photograph	50
Praxair, Inc.	PX	NYSE	Industrial Gases	54
Procter & Gamble	PG	NYSE	Consumer Products	52

Company	Symbol	Exchange	Business	% of Revenues (from overseas)
Raychem	RYC	NYSE	Plastics for Electronics	62
Rayonier	RYN	NYSE	Timber Products	50
Reader's Digest	RDA	NYSE	Publishing	60
Reading & Bates	RB	NYSE	Contract Offshore Drilling	88
Robotic Vision Systems	ROBV	Nasdaq	Aircraft Ice Detectors	62
Roper Industries	ROPR	Nasdaq	Fluid-Handling Products	52
STM Wireless, Inc.	STMI	Nasdaq	Satellite Communications	70
Schulman (A.), Inc.	SHLM	Nasdaq	High-Performance Resins	57
Smith International	SII	NYSE	Drilling Tools	50
Sola International	SOL	NYSE	Eyeglass Lenses	50
Standard Commercial	STW	NYSE	Leaf Tobacco	74
Summagraphics	SUGR	Nasdaq	Computer Peripherals	53
Tektronix, Inc.	TEK	NYSE	Electronic Instrumentation	50
3Com Corp.	COMS	Nasdaq	Computer Networks	54
Trimble Navigation	TRMB	Nasdaq	Satellite Position Finding	50
Unitrode Corp.	UTR	NYSE	Electronic Components	56
Varco International	VRC	NYSE	Drilling Products	68
WMS Industries	WMS	NYSE	Games	51
Wahlco Environmental	WAL	NYSE	Air-Pollution Control	51
Warner-Lambert	WLA	NYSE	Pharmaceuticals	54
Weatherford International	WII	NYSE	Energy Service	50
Worldtex, Inc.	WTX	NYSE	Specialty Yarns	59
Xicor, Inc.	XICO	Nasdaq	Semiconductor Memory	50
Zilog, Inc.	ZLOG	Nasdaq	Integrated Circuits	51

◆ APPENDIX G ◆

Direct Investments in Foreign Securities

The following list of ADRs, ADSs, GDSs, and ordinary shares (common stock) is organized by country. However, because many of these companies are global in their operations, do not assume that their business results exactly match the performance of the country's economy. This partial list, intended to provide an indication of the availability of foreign companies to the U.S. investor, is not a recommendation to buy any security. Both the New York Stock Exchange (NYSE) and the American Stock Exchange (AMEX) provide complete lists of all ADRs traded on their floors. The Washington, D.C., office of the National Association of Security Dealers (NASD) will supply the names of Nasdaq traded ADRs, along with many that are traded over the counter.

Note: 1. A superscript following the company name indicates the sponsor of a dividend reinvestment plan for the ADR or ADS as follows: [BNY] for Bank of New York; [MGT] for Morgan Guaranty Trust.

Note: 2. Exchange listings are abbreviated as follows: NYSE for New York Stock Exchange, Nasdaq for National Association of Security Dealers, and OTC for Over-the-Counter Market.

Argentina

Company Name	Symbol	Exchange	Number of Shares	Business
IRSA Inversiones y Representa	IRS	NYSE	ADS = 10	Real Estate
YPF Sociedad Anónima^{BNY}	YPF	NYSE	ADR = 1 D	Integrated Petroleum
Banco Francés Rio de la Plata	BFR	NYSE	ADS = 3	Banking
Telecom Argentina^{MGT}	TEO	NYSE	ADS = 10 B	Telephones

Australia

Company Name	Symbol	Exchange	Number of Shares	Business
Coles Myer, Ltd.	CM	NYSE	ADS = 8	Retail Stores
FAI Insurance, Ltd.	FAI	NYSE	ADS = 20	Insurance
Lihir Gold^{BNY}	LIHRY	Nasdaq	ADR = 20	Gold Mining
National Australia Bank	NAB	NYSE	ADR = 5	Commercial Bank
News Corp., Ltd.	NWS	NYSE	ADS = 8	Publishing
Orbital Engine Co.	OE	NYSE	ADS = 8	Two-Stroke Engines
WMC, Ltd.	WMC	NYSE	ADR = 4	Gold, Petroleum
Westpac Banking, Ltd.^{MGT}	WBK	NYSE	ADS = 5	Banking

Belgium

Company Name	Symbol	Exchange	Number of Shares	Business
Fortis AG	AGFIB	OTC	Ordinary	Banking, Insurance

Bolivia

Company Name	Symbol	Exchange	Number of Shares	Business
Boliviana de Energia	BLP	NYSE	ADS = 1	Electric Utility

Brazil

Company Name	Symbol	Exchange	Number of Shares	Business
Aracruz Celulose, S.A.	ARA	NYSE	ADS = 5 B	Paper Mfg.
Companhia Energética de Sao Paulo	CESSA	OTC	ADS = 10	Hydroelectric

Chile

Company Name	Symbol	Exchange	Number of Shares	Business
Banco de A. Edwards	AED	NYSE	ADS = 165 A	Banking
Banco O'Higgins	OHG	NYSE	ADS = 6	Banking
Banco Osomo	BOU	NYSE	ADS = 220 A	Banking
Chilgener, S.A.	CHR	NYSE	ADS = 4	Electric Utility
Compania de Telefonos de Chile	CTC	NYSE	ADS = 17	Telecommunications
Empresas Telex-Chile, S.A.	TL	NYSE	ADS = 2	Telecommunications
Maderas y Sintéticos	MYS	NYSE	ADS = 30	Particle Board
Sociedad Quimica	SQM	NYSE	ADS = 10	Fertilizers

China

Company Name	Symbol	Exchange	Number of Shares	Business
China Yuchai International	CYD	NYSE	Ordinary	Diesel Engines
Huaneng Power International	HNP	NYSE	ADS = 40 N	Electric Power
Jilin Chemical Industrial	JCC	NYSE	ADS = 100	Chemicals
Shanghai Petrochemical	SHI	NYSE	ADS = 100	Petroleum

Colombia

Company Name	Symbol	Exchange	Number of Shares	Business
Banco Granadero, S.A.	BGA	NYSE	ADS = 100	Banking

Denmark

Company Name	Symbol	Exchange	Number of Shares	Business
Novo Nordisk[MGT]	NVO	NYSE	ADS = 0.2	Industrial Enzymes

France

Company Name	Symbol	Exchange	Number of Shares	Business
Alcatel Alsthom	ALA	NYSE	ADS = 0.2	Telecom-munications
Elf Aquitaime	ELF	NYSE	ADS = 0.5	Integrated Oil
Flamel Technologies, S.A.[BNY]	FLMLY	Nasdaq	ADS = 1	Pharma-cuetical
Groupe AB[BNY]	ABG	NYSE	ADR = 0.5	TV Programing
Rhone-Poulenc	RP	NYSE	ADS = 1	Chemicals
SCOR[BNY]	SCO	NYSE	ADR = 1	Reinsurance
SGS-Thomson Electronics	STM	NYSE	Global Share	Semi-conductors
TOTAL	TOT	NYSE	ADS = 0.5	Integrated Oil

Germany

Company Name	Symbol	Exchange	Number of Shares	Business
Dailmer-Benz AG	DAI	NYSE	ADS = 0.1	Automotive
Fresenius Medical[MGT]	FMS	NYSE	3 ADS = 1	Medical Diagnostics

Great Britain

Company Name	Symbol	Exchange	Number of Shares	Business
Amvescap PLC[MGT]	AVZ	NYSE	ADR = 10	Fund Management
Barclays PLC[MGT]	BCS	NYSE	ADS = 4	Banking
British Telecommuni-cations[MGT]	BTY	NYSE	ADR = 10	Telephones
Cadbury Schweppes[MGT]	CADEY	Nasdaq	ADS = 10	Soft Drinks, Candy
Grand Metropolitan[MGT]	GRM	NYSE	ADS = 4	Food, Wine, Spirits

Company Name	Symbol	Exchange	Number of Shares	Business
Huntingdon Life Sciences[BNY]	HTD	NYSE	ADR = 5	Biosafety Testing
Imperial Chemical Industries PLC[MGT]	ICI	NYSE	ADR = 4	Chemicals
London International Group PLC[BNY]	LONDY	Nasdaq	ADR = 5	Health Products
Micro Focus Group PLC[BNY]	MIFGY	Nasdaq	ADR = 1	Program Software
National Westminster Bank[MGT]	NW	NYSE	ADR = 1	Retail Banking
Power Generation PLC	PWG	NYSE	ADS = 4	Electric Generation
Rank Group PLC[MGT]	RANKY	Nasdaq	ADR = 2	Film, TV
Reuters Holdings PLC[MGT]	RTRSY	Nasdaq	ADS = 6	Electronic Publishing
Small World PLC[BNY]	SWLDY	Nasdaq	ADS = 1	Computer Software
Thom PLC[MGT]	THRNY	Nasdaq	ADR = 4	Retail Electronics
Unilever PLC[MGT]	UL	NYSE	ADS = 4	Consumer Products
Unionamerica Holdings PLC[MGT]	UA	NYSE	ADR = 1	Reinsurance
Willis Corroon Group PLC	WCG	NYSE	ADS = 5	Insurance
Zeneca Group PLC[MGT]	ZEN	NYSE	ADS = 3	Pharmaceutical

Hong Kong

Company Name	Symbol	Exchange	Number of Shares	Business
Asia Satellite Telecom[MGT]	SAT	NYSE	ADR = 10	Satellite Relays
Bonso Electronics	BONSOF	Nasdaq	Ordinary	Electronic Scales
C.P. Pokphand	CPPKY	OTC	ADS = 25	International Trading
Dairy Farm International	DFIH	OTC	ADS = 25	Fast Foods
Hong Kong Telecom	HKT	NYSE	ADS = 10	Telephones
Universal Matchbox Group, Ltd.	UMG	NYSE	Ordinary	Toys

Ireland

Company Name	Symbol	Exchange	Number of Shares	Business
Allied Irish Banks PLC	AIB	NYSE	ADS = 6	International Banking
Elan Corporation PLC	ELN	NYSE	ADS = 1	Pharmaceutical
Saville Systems PLC[BNY]	SAVLY	Nasdaq	ADR = 1	Office Billing Systems
Waterford Wedgewood[MGT]	WATFZ	Nasdaq	ADS = 10	Tableware, Crystal

Israel

Company Name	Symbol	Exchange	Number of Shares	Business
Blue Square-Israel, Ltd.[BNY]	BSI	NYSE	ADR = 1	Retail Stores
ECI Telecom	ECILF	Nasdaq	Ordinary	Digital Circuits
Koor Industries, Ltd.[BNY]	KOR	NYSE	ADR = 5	Telecom-munications
Matav-Cable Systems Media[BNY]	MATVY	Nasdaq	ADS = 2	TV Cable
PEC Israel Economic	IEC	NYSE	Ordinary	Business Development
Tadiran, Ltd.	TAD	NYSE	Ordinary	Telecom-munications Equipment
Taro Pharmaceutical Industries	TAROF	Nasdaq	Ordinary	Pharmaceutical

Italy

Company Name	Symbol	Exchange	Number of Shares	Business
De Rigo S.P.A.[BNY]	DER	NYSE	ADR = 1	Sunglasses
Fiat S.P.A.[MGT]	FIA	NYSE	ADR = 5	Automobiles
Industric Natuzzi S.P.A.	NTZ	NYSE	ADS = 1	Leather Goods
Instituto Mobiliare Italiano	IMI	NYSE	ADS = 3	Banking
Luxottica Group S.P.A.[BNY]	LUX	NYSE	ADS = 1	Eyeglass Frames
Montedison S.P.A.	MNT	NYSE	ADS = 10	Chemicals

Japan

Company Name	Symbol	Exchange	Number of Shares	Business
Amway Japan, Ltd.[MGT]	AJL	NYSE	ADS = 0.5	Distributer
Bank of Tokyo-Mitsubishi[BNY]	MBK	NYSE	ADS = 1	International Banking
Canon, Inc.	CANNY	Nasdaq	ADR = 5	Photographic Equipment
Fuji Heavy Industries	FUJHY	OTC	ADR = 10	Auto, Aircraft
Hitachi, Ltd.	HIT	NYSE	ADR = 10	Heavy Industrial
Kubota Corp.	KUB	NYSE	ADS = 20	Farm Equipment
Kyocera Corp.	KYO	NYSE	ADS = 2	Ceramics, Electronics
Makita[BNY]	MKTAY	Nasdaq	ADS = 1	Portable Tools
Matsushita Bank	MBK	NYSE	ADR = 1	Banking
Matsushita Electronics	MC	NYSE	ADS = 10	Electronics
NEC Corp.[BNY]	NIPNY	Nasdaq	ADR = 5	Computers
Nippon Telephone[MGT]	NTT	NYSE	ADR = 1	Telephone
Nissan Motors	NSANY	Nasdaq	ADR = 10	Automobiles
Pioneer Electronics	PIO	NYSE	ADS = 1	Consumer Electronics
Ricoh	RICOY	OTC	ADR = 5	Office Automation
Sanyo Electric	SANYY	Nasdaq	ADR = 5	Video Equipment
Sony Corp.[MGT]	SNE	NYSE	ADS = 1	Electronics
TDK Corp.[MGT]	TDK	NYSE	ADS = 1	Magnetic Recording
Toyota Motors	TOYOY	Nasdaq	ADR = 2	Automobiles

Korea

Company Name	Symbol	Exchange	Number of Shares	Business
Korea Electric Power	KEP	NYSE	ADS = 0.5	Electric Utility

Mexico

Company Name	Symbol	Exchange	Number of Shares	Business
Coca-Cola FEMSA, S.A.	KOF	NYSE	ADS = 10	Coke Bottler
Cemex SA de CV	CMXBY	OTC	ADS = 2	Cement, Concrete
Empresas ICA-Soe[BNY]	ICA	NYSE	ADS = 1	Highway Construction
Empresas La Moderna[BNY]	ELM	NYSE	ADS = 4	Cigarettes
Grupo Casa Autrey, S.A.[MGT]	ARY	NYSE	ADS = 10	Beauty Products
Grupo Embotellador	GEM	NYSE	GDS = 2	Pepsi Bottler
Grupa Financial Serfin	SFN	NYSE	ADR = 4	Commercial Bank
Grupo Mex de Des	GMD	NYSE	ADR = 1	Highway Construction
Grupo Telvisa	TV	NYSE	GDS = 2	TV Programs
Grupo Tribasa	GTR	NYSE	ADR = 2	Construction
Teléfonos de Mexico	TMX	NYSE	ADS = 1	Telephone
Transportación Marítima	TMM	NYSE	ADS = 1	Shipping
Tubos de Acero de Mexico[MGT]	TAM	NYSE	ADR = 1	Steel Pipe
Vitro Sociedad Amonima	VTO	NYSE	ADS = 3	Glass

The Netherlands

Company Name	Symbol	Exchange	Number of Shares	Business
AEGON, N.V.[MGT]	AEG	NYSE	Ordinary	Insurance
Akzo Nobel, N.V.[MGT]	AKZOY	Nasdaq	ADR = 0.5	Chemicals
Koninklijke Ahold, N.V.[MGT]	AHO	NYSE	ADS = 1	Retail Food
Oce-Van Der Grinten, N.V.[MGT]	OCENY	Nasdaq	ADR = 0.2	Copy Equipment
Poly Gram, N.V.	PLG	NYSE	Ordinary	Recordings
Royal Dutch Petroleum[MGT]	RD	NYSE	Ordinary	Integrated Oil
Singer Company, N.V.	SEW	NYSE	Ordinary	Sewing Machines
Unilever, N.V. [MGT]	UN	NYSE	Ordinary	Consumer Products

Norway

Company Name	Symbol	Exchange	Number of Shares	Business
Nera A.S.[BNY]	NERAY	Nasdaq	ADS = 1	Telecom-munications Equipment
Norsk Hydro, A.S.[MGT]	NHY	NYSE	ADS = 1	Fertilizers

Peru

Company Name	Symbol	Exchange	Number of Shares	Business
Banco Wiese[MGT]	BWP	NYSE	ADS = 4	Banking
Telefonica del Peru[MGT]	TDP	NYSE	ADS = 10 B	Telephone

Philippines

Company Name	Symbol	Exchange	Number of Shares	Business
Philippine Long Distance	PHI	NYSE	ADS = 1	Telephone

Portugal

Company Name	Symbol	Exchange	Number of Shares	Business
Banco Comercial Portugues	BPC	NYSE	ADS = 1	Banking
Portugal Telecom, S.A.	PT	NYSE	ADS = 1	Telephone

Russia

Company Name	Symbol	Exchange	Number of Shares	Business
Vimpel Communications[BNY]	VIP	NYSE	ADS = 0.75	Cellular Telephone

Spain

Company Name	Symbol	Exchange	Number of Shares	Business
Banco Bilbao Vizcaya	BBV	NYSE	ADS = 1	Commercial Bank
Banco Central	BCH	NYSE	Ordinary	Banking
Banco Santander[MGT]	STD	NYSE	ADS = 1	Bank Holding Company
Corporacion Bancaria[MGT]	AGR	NYSE	ADS = 0.5	Banking
Empresa Nacional Electricidad[MGT]	ELE	NYSE	ADS = 1	Electric Utility
Repsol, S.A.[BNY]	REP	NYSE	ADS = 1	Crude Oil, Natural Gas
Telefónica de Espana	TEF	NYSE	ADS = 3	Telephone

Sweden

Company Name	Symbol	Exchange	Number of Shares	Business
Aktiebolaget Svensk ExportKredit	SEP PR	NYSE	1 Pfd. Stock	Export Finance
Volvo AB	VOLVY	Nasdaq	ADR = 1	Autos, Trucks

Switzerland

Company Name	Symbol	Exchange	Number of Shares	Business
Adecco, S.A.[MGT]	ADECY	Nasdaq	ADR = 0.125	Temporary Help
Nestle, S.A.	NSRGY	OTC	ADR = 0.05	Chocolate, Foods
Novartis	NVTSY	OTC	ADR = 0.05	Pharmaceutical
Tag Heuer International, S.A.[MGT]	THW	NYSE	ADS = 0.1	Sport Watches

Venezuela

Company Name	Symbol	Exchange	Number of Shares	Business
Able Telecom Holding	ABTE	Nasdaq	Ordinary	Telephone
Corimon C.A.	CMR	NYSE	ADR = 35	Paint Manufacture
Mavesa[BNY]	MAV	NYSE	ADR = 40	Food Products

Currencies of the World
(as of December 31, 1997)

Country	Local Currency
Afghanistan	afghani
Albania	lek
Algeria	Algerian dinar
American Samoa	U.S. dollar
Andorra	Spanish peseta
Angola	kwanza
Anguilla	East Caribbean dollar
Antigua/Barbuda	East Caribbean dollar
Armenia	ruble
Argentina	austral
Aruba	Aruban florin
Australia	Australian dollar
Austria	schilling
Bahamas	Bahamian dollar
Bahrain	Bahrain dinar
Bangladesh	taka
Barbados	Barbados dollar
Belgium	Belgian franc
Belize	Belizean dollar
Benin	CFA franc
Bermuda	Bermuda dollar

Country	Local Currency
Belarus	Belarus ruble
Bhutan	ngultrum
Bolivia	boliviano
Bosnia	dinar
Botswana	pula
Brazil	new cruzado
Brunei	Brunei dollar
Bulgaria	lev
Burkina	CFA franc
(Burma) Myanmar	kyat
Burundi	Burundi franc
Cameroon	CFA franc
Canada	Canadian dollar
Cape Verde	Cape Verde escudo
Cayman Islands	Cayman Islands dollar
Central African Republic	CFA franc
Chad	CFA franc
Chile	Chilean peso
China	yuan
Christmas Island	Australian dollar
Cocos Island	Australian dollar
Colombia	Colombian peso
Comoros	Comorian franc
Congo	CFA franc
Cook Island	Australian dollar
Costa Rico	Costa Rican colón
Côte d'Ivoire	CFA franc
Croatia	Croatian dinar
Cuba	Cuban peso
Cyprus	Cyprian pound
Czech Republic	koruna
Democratic Republic of Congo	zaire
Denmark	Danish krone
Djibouti	Djiboutin franc
Dominica	East Caribbean dollar
Dominican Republic	Dominican Republic peso
East Timor	Indonesian rupiah
Ecuador	sucre

Country	Local Currency
Egypt	Egyptian pound
El Salvador	El Salvador colon
Estonia	kroon
Ethiopia	birr
Falkland Islands	Falkland Islands pound
Faroes	Faroese krone
Fiji	Fiji dollar
Finland	markka
France	French franc
French Guiana	French franc
French Polynesia	CFP franc
Gabon	CFA franc
Gambia	dalasi
Georgia	ruble
Germany	deutsche mark
Ghana	cedi
Gibralter	Gibralter pound
Greece	drachma
Greenland	Danish krone
Grenada	East Caribbean dollar
Guadeloupe	French franc
Guam	U.S. dollar
Guatemala	quetzal
Guernsey	Guernsey pound
Guinea	Guinean franc
Guyana	Guyanese dollar
Haiti	gourde
Honduras	lempira
Hong Kong	Hong Kong dollar
Hungary	florint
Iceland	Icelandic krona
India	Indian rupee
Indonesia	rupiah
Iran	rial
Iraq	Iraqi dinar
Ireland	Irish pound
Isle of Man	U.K. pound
Israel	shekel

Country	Local Currency
Italy	lira
Jamaica	Jamaican dollar
Japan	yen
Jersey	U.K. pound
Johnston Island	U.S. dollar
Jordan	Jordan dinar
Kampuchea	riel
Kenya	Kenyan shilling
Kiribati	Australian dollar
Kuwait	Kuwaiti dinar
Laos	kip
Latvia	lats
Lebanon	Lebanese pound
Lesotho	loti
Liberia	Liberian dollar
Libya	Libyan dinar
Liechtenstein	Swiss franc
Lithuania	litas
Luxembourg	Luxembourg franc
Macao	patacea
Madagascar	Madagascar franc
Malawi	kwacha
Malaysia	ringgit
Maldives	rufiyaa
Mali	CFA franc
Malta	Maltese lira
Martinique	French franc
Mauritania	ouguiya
Mauritius	Mauritius rupee
Mayotte	French franc
Mexico	Mexican peso
Midway Island	U.S. dollar
Moldova	leu
Monaco	French franc
Mongolia	tugrik
Montserrat	East Caribbean dollar
Morocco	dirham
Mozambique	metical

Country	Local Currency
Myanmar (Burma)	kyat
Nambia	South African rand
Nauru	Australian dollar
Nepal	Nepalese rupee
Netherlands	guilder
Netherlands Antilles	North Antilles guilder
New Caledonia	CFP franc
New Zealand	New Zealand dollar
Nicaragua	córdoba
Niger	CFA franc
Nigeria	naira
Niue	New Zealand dollar
Norfolk Island	Australian dollar
North Korea	North Korean won
North Yemen	North Yemen rial
Norway	Norwegian krone
Oman	Omani rial
Pakistan	Pakistan rupee
Panama	balboa
Papua New Guinea	kina
Paraguay	guarani
Peru	inti
Philippines	Philippine peso
Pitcairn Island	New Zealand dollar
Poland	zloty
Portugal	escudo
Puerto Rico	U.S. dollar
Qatar	Qatar riyal
Réunion	French franc
Romania	leu
Russia	ruble
Rwanda	Rwandan franc
Sahara, Western	Moroccan dirham
St. Christopher	East Caribbean dollar
Ste. Helena	Ste. Helena pound
Ste. Lucia	East Caribbean dollar
St. Pierre & Miquelon	French franc
St. Vincent	East Caribbean dollar

Country	Local Currency
San Marino	San Marino lira
Sao Tomé	dobra
Saudi Arabia	Saudi riyal
Senegal	CFA franc
Seychelles	Seychelles rupee
Sierra Leone	leone
Singapore	Singapore dollar
Slovakia	koruna
Slovenia	tolar
Soloman Islands	Soloman Islands dollar
Somalia	Somalia shilling
South Africa	rand
South Korea	South Korean won
South Yemen	South Yemen dinar
Spain	peseta
Sri Lanka	Sri Lanka rupee
Sudan	Sudanese pound
Surinam	Surinam guilder
Swaziland	lilangeni
Sweden	Swedish krona
Switzerland	Swiss franc
Syria	Syrian pound
Taiwan	New Taiwan dollar
Tanzania	Tanzanian shilling
Thailand	baht
Togo	CFA franc
Tokelau	New Zealand dollar
Tonga	pa'anga
Trinidad/Tobago	Trinidad/Tobago dollar
Tunisia	Tunisian dinar
Turkey	Turkish lira
Turks/Caicos Islands	U.S. dollar
Tuvalu	Tuvaluan dollar
Uganda	Uganda new shilling
Ukraine	hryvna
United Arab Emirates	U.A.E. dirham
United Kingdom	Pound sterling
United States	U.S. dollar

Country	Local Currency
Uruguay	Uruguay peso
Vanuatu	vatu
Vatican	Vatican City lira
Venezuela	bolivar
Vietnam	dông
Virgin Islands	U.S. dollar
Wake Island	U.S. dollar
Wallis/Futuna	CFP franc
Western Samoa	West Samoan tala
Zambia	kwacha
Zimbabwe	Zimbabwe dollar

◆ G L O S S A R Y ◆

accumulate Adding to positions, usually over a long period of time.

ask An offer to sell a security at a specified price.

arbitrage The purchase and sale of identical items in different markets to profit from temporary price differentials between those markets.

bear A person expecting lower prices.

bear market Any market in which prices are declining over a period of time.

bid An offer to buy a security at a specified price.

broker One who acts to bring together a buyer with a seller.

bull A person expecting higher prices.

bull market Any market in which prices are trending upward over a period of time.

call option The right to buy a specified item (stock, real estate, commodity futures, etc.) at a fixed price at any time during a set period of time.

contract The unit of trading for a commodity future.

cover To close out a position (short-sale, option, futures, etc.) through an opposite transaction.

credit An entry stating money owed to a customer's account. A credit balance represents money that is available for withdrawal.

day-trade A transaction that includes a buy and sell on the same day. A day-trade requires only maintenance margin and often receives a lower commission charge.

debit An entry stating charges against a customer's account. A debit balance represents money that is owed.

delivery The fulfillment of a futures contract through the tender and receipt of the actual commodity.

discount The amount by which something is priced at less than intrinsic value.

down-tick A trade at a price below the preceding trade.

equity Common stock representing ownership; the net value of an account after all debits have been subtracted from the total value of the account.

excess Equity exceeding initial margin requirements. Withdrawal of excess will increase a debit balance.

forward contract A contract with a bank for a specified sum of a foreign currency to be settled on a specified date in the future.

GATT The General Agreement on Tariffs and Trade, founded in 1948 to establish a code of conduct for international trade, to reduce tariffs through multilateral agreements, and to constitute a forum for the resolution of trade disputes.

hedge To assume positions in such a way that the market risk is neutral (i.e., sell 100 shares of a stock and buy a call option on the same stock).

IMF International Monetary Fund, a specialized agency of the United Nations that allows members to borrow from the fund to counter financial emergencies.

intrinsic value The difference between the market price of a stock and the exercise price of a related option.

limit The specified price at which an order is to be executed if possible. Also, an arbitrary figure, set by an exchange, beyond which no trades may be executed until the following day.

liquidation The process of balancing or closing out either a long or short position.

long A position of ownership. One is long in expectation of a price increase.

margin (initial) The amount of money a customer must deposit when buying on credit. Currently, 50 percent of the market value of the security purchased is required.

margin (maintenance) The amount of equity required to maintain positions. Currently, 30 percent of total market value is required for security accounts.

market A central place where orders are executed. Also, an order for immediate execution at the best price available at the time.

naked An unhedged position.

peg To maintain the value of a local currency in terms of one of the major currencies. To peg the Hong Kong dollar to the U.S. dollar means that the relationship is held steady through open market buying and selling of the two currencies.

premium The amount by which something is valued above its intrinsic value.

short The sale of a security that one does not own with the hope of profiting from a decline in market value, at which time the sale may be covered.

speculator One who assesses current conditions to anticipate price changes that will position capital to obtain gains.

spot market A market in which trades are settled immediately.

straddle A hedging combination of a put and a call option on the same security.

strike price The exercise price of an option.

up-tick A trade at a price higher than the preceding trade.

WEBS World Equity Benchmark Shares, closed-end index funds designed to track the performance of the equity market in a single country.

World Bank A United Nations agency that assists underdeveloped nations to improve living conditions through loans for long-term projects in transportation, energy, agriculture, etc.

WTO The World Trade Organization, founded in 1995 to replace GATT as the regulatory body of international trade.

◆ INDEX ◆

4-Week Free Trial

Four weeks of unbiased, exceptional coverage of world business news — FREE. Subscribe to the FINANCIAL TIMES today and get the news and information you need to stay on top of what's happening in the world.

The FINANCIAL TIMES gives you the edge you need to succeed in the global marketplace. It's the single source of in-depth world news and information you require. Six days-a-week you'll get the inside story on emerging markets, business, government, management and technology, delivered to your home or office. And our U.S. edition gives a fresh perspective on the stories and topics of interest to American readers.

Subscribe to the one newspaper more business leaders rely on everyday. The FINANCIAL TIMES.

To order, call
800-628-8088

FINANCIAL TIMES
The global daily of business

FREE TRIAL CERTIFICATE

☐ **Yes,** Send me the FINANCIAL TIMES six days a week (Monday through Saturday) for the next four weeks free. If I like it, I'll continue to receive 48 more weeks (for a total of 52 weeks in all) with a one year subscription for just $184 when you bill me later. That's only 60 cents per issue – a saving of 40% off the cover price. If I decide it's not for me, I'll write "cancel" on your invoice, return it and owe nothing. The free issues are mine to keep without any further obligation.

Name _____

Company/Title _____

Address/Apt./Floor/Suite _____

City/State/Zip _____

Telephone/Fax (optional) _____

For immediate service call **800-628-8088**
Fax: **212-308-2397**, or mail, FINANCIAL TIMES, 14 East 60th Street, New York, NY 10022
E-mail: uscirculation@FT.com
Limited time offer. Good for new subscribers in the U.S. only.

SA148

DATE DUE

DEC 29 1998	
JAN 1 9 1999	
JAN 2 8 1999	
FEB 1 5 1999	
MAR 2 0 1999	
MAR 2 7 1999	
JUN 1 1 1999	
DEC 0 8 1999	
JAN 0 4 2000	
APR 2 7 2009	

GAYLORD   PRINTED IN U.S.A.